T0006615

A GIFT FOR: _____

FROM: _____

DATE: _____

DANGEROUS
FAITH

50 POWERFUL BELIEVERS

Who Changed THE WORLD

Compiled by Susan Hill

Portrait illustrations by Darko Stojanovic

THOMAS NELSON
Since 1798

Dangerous Faith

© 2022 Thomas Nelson

All rights reserved. No portion of this book may be reproduced, stored in a retrieval system, or transmitted in any form or by any means—electronic, mechanical, photocopy, recording, scanning, or other—except for brief quotations in critical reviews or articles, without the prior written permission of the publisher.

Published in Nashville, Tennessee, by Thomas Nelson. Thomas Nelson is a registered trademark of HarperCollins Christian Publishing, Inc.

Compiled by Susan Hill

Illustrations by Darko Stojanovic

Unless otherwise noted, Scripture quotations are taken from the ESV® Bible (The Holy Bible, English Standard Version®). Copyright © 2001 by Crossway, a publishing ministry of Good News Publishers. Used by permission. All rights reserved.

Scripture quotations marked NIV are taken from the Holy Bible, New International Version®, NIV®. Copyright © 1973, 1978, 1984, 2011 by Biblica, Inc.® Used by permission of Zondervan. All rights reserved worldwide. www.zondervan.com. The "NIV" and "New International Version" are trademarks registered in the United States Patent and Trademark Office by Biblica, Inc.®

Scripture quotations marked NKJV are taken from the New King James Version®. Copyright © 1982 by Thomas Nelson. Used by permission. All rights reserved.

Thomas Nelson titles may be purchased in bulk for educational, business, fundraising, or sales promotional use. For information, please e-mail SpecialMarkets@ThomasNelson.com.

Any internet addresses, phone numbers, or company or product information printed in this book are offered as a resource and are not intended in any way to be or to imply an endorsement by Thomas Nelson, nor does Thomas Nelson vouch for the existence, content, or services of these sites, phone numbers, companies, or products beyond the life of this book.

ISBN 978-1-4002-3288-8 (audiobook)
ISBN 978-1-4002-3284-0 (eBook)
ISBN 978-1-4002-3287-1 (HC)

Printed in India

22 23 24 25 26   REP   10 9 8 7 6 5 4 3 2 1

CONTENTS

SUSAN B. ANTHONY

(1820–1906)

❦

As a young girl Anthony was guided by the Quaker belief that everyone is equal under God. Born to Daniel and Lucy Adams on February 15, 1820, in Adams, Massachusetts, she came from a family with seven siblings, many of whom became activists of justice and worked on behalf of the emancipation of slaves.[1]

Anthony spent several years teaching, and when she returned to her family, she met Frederick Douglass and William Lloyd Garrison, who were friends of her father. Listening to them speak motivated Anthony to do more to end slavery. At the time it was considered inappropriate for women to give speeches in public. Despite the social stigma Anthony became an abolition activist and spoke publicly against slavery.

In 1851 Anthony met and became good friends with Elizabeth Cady Stanton. The two spent the next five decades traveling the country fighting for women's rights. Anthony's speeches calling

for a woman's right to vote put her at risk for being arrested. Together, Anthony and Stanton founded the American Equal Rights Association, and they became editors of *The Revolution,* the association's newspaper that communicated the ideals of equality and rights for women. Anthony became well known as she continued to speak to raise money to publish the paper and support the organization. Public opinion was divided about her. She was well respected by some and despised by others.

In 1872 Anthony brought national attention to the suffrage movement when she was arrested for voting. She was convicted and fined one hundred dollars. Anthony never married, and she dedicated her life to working for women's rights. In 1906 at the age of eighty-six, Anthony died of heart failure and pneumonia. It would be another fourteen years before the Nineteenth Amendment was passed, giving women the right to vote. When it finally came to pass, it was nicknamed the "Susan B. Anthony Amendment" in her honor. In 1979 the United States Treasury Department recognized her dedication and achievement by putting her portrait on one-dollar coins—she was the first woman to achieve this distinction.

"I distrust those people
who know so well what God
wants them to do, because
I notice it always coincides
with their own desires."

SUSAN B. ANTHONY[2]

ANNE ASKEW

1521–1546

Anne Askew was vocal about her religious conviction during a time in history when women were expected to remain silent. Born in 1521 the daughter of a knighted member of Parliament, Askew could've easily chosen a life of frivolous leisure. But she was passionate about the Holy Scriptures and sharing her faith. As a result she was imprisoned, illegally tortured, and ultimately burned at the stake.[1]

During the Protestant Reformation, Askew spoke out against the Catholic doctrine of transubstantiation—the doctrine that teaches that during Mass, the elements of bread and wine convert into the actual body and blood of Christ. Askew asserted that the bread and wine served only as a symbol of remembrance of Christ. She also insisted the Word of God is the ultimate authority in matters of faith and practice. In London, Askew was outspoken in sharing the gospel and earned the name "Fair Gospeller."[2]

She was arrested on more than one occasion and was released each time. But King Henry VIII had no tolerance for Protestant Reformers, and under his rule he had enough to convict Askew of heresy.[3]

Askew was brought into custody and taken to the Tower of London, where she was tortured by being placed on a rack. The rack was a torture device used to get victims to recant their faith and provide names of others who believed the same. On the rack Askew was bound to a wooden frame and fastened to rollers designed to pull her limbs in opposite directions—ultimately pulling her arms, legs, hips, and shoulders out of their sockets as well as pulling muscles and ligaments beyond repair. Despite being permanently disabled, Askew refused to recant her faith and didn't give up a single name. No longer able to walk, Askew was carried back to her prison cell. Seventeen days later—at the age of twenty-five—she was burned at the stake for her faith.

Askew spoke and wrote courageously about her faith and lived out her belief until her death. When convicted of heresy she accepted her sentence quietly. Before her death, she declined to speak with a priest for confession, stating she would confess her sins directly to God and was confident she would be forgiven.

"Then they did put me on the rack, because I confessed no ladies or gentlemen, to be of my opinion . . . the Lord Chancellor and Master Rich took pains to rack me with their own hands, till I was nearly dead. I fainted . . . and then they recovered me again."

Anne Askew[4]

ELIZABETH BLACKWELL

1821–1910

~~~❦~~~

Elizabeth Blackwell was the first woman to receive a medical degree in the United States. Born in Bristol, England, to Samuel Blackwell and Hannah Lane, she was the third of nine children. Her younger sister Emily would become the third woman to receive her medical degree in America and the first female surgeon.

In 1832 the Blackwell family moved to America amid the cholera epidemic. Early on Blackwell had no desire to study medicine but was drawn to literature and philosophy. But when a dying friend suggested her ordeal would've been easier if she'd had a female physician, Blackwell was inspired to pursue her medical degree.[1] She sent out dozens of applications, and each

one was promptly denied because of her gender. She was told her hopes to become a doctor were admirable but impossible.

Despite a stack of rejected applications, Blackwell believed she had been divinely sanctioned to study medicine. She'd been raised in a deeply religious family, and her faith motivated her desire to dedicate her life to serving others. Blackwell thought that "women could be anything they wished according to the limits of individual talent and toil, and in reaching their fullest potential would raise humanity closer to its ideal."[2] In 1847 Blackwell applied to Geneva Medical College. The faculty dean, Charles A. Lee, asked the student body to vote and stated that she would be denied entrance if even one of the 113 male students voted against her admission. The student body viewed the vote as a joke—never believing it would be a reality—and unanimously voted her in. Two years later in 1849, Blackwell graduated first in her class.

In 1857 Elizabeth opened the New York Infirmary for Women and Children with her sister Dr. Emily Blackwell. Their mission was to provide medical care for the poor and training for female physicians. The Blackwell sisters died in 1910. There were more than nine thousand female physicians in America at the time of their passing—roughly 6 percent of all doctors. Today, 35 percent of medical doctors are women, and slightly more than half of all medical students are women.[3]

"My whole life is devoted
unreservedly to the service of
my sex. The study and practice
of medicine is in my thought but
one means to a great end . . . the
true ennoblement of woman."

ELIZABETH BLACKWELL[4]

WILLIAM BOOTH

1829–1912

⁓⟐⁓

Williams Booth was referred to as "The Prophet of the Poor" and is best known as the founder of the Salvation Army. Booth was born into a poor family in Nottingham, England, where his parents were on the low end of the working-class population. When Booth was fourteen his father died, and it fell to the teenager to earn money to support the family. Shortly after his father's passing, Booth was invited to attend a chapel, and it was then he became a Christian. After his conversion he wrote in his diary, "God shall have all there is of William Booth."[1]

In 1852 Booth began his ministerial career. In London he walked the streets preaching to the marginalized, poor, and destitute. When Booth's fellow ministers disagreed with Booth's approach to ministry, Booth had to decide whether he would remain in a traditional pastoral role or take a riskier path by carving out his own type of ministry. He asked, "Why all this

apparatus of temples and meeting-houses to save men from perdition in a world which is to come, while never a helping hand is stretched out to save them from the inferno of their present life?"[2]

Booth and his wife, Catherine, withdrew from traditional church ministry for the unconventional approach of taking the gospel of Jesus Christ directly to the people. They also began training evangelists throughout England.[3] Initially Booth's organization was called the Christian Mission. Within the first decade they recruited and trained more than one thousand volunteers and evangelists. In 1878 Booth changed the name to the Salvation Army. They continued to preach the gospel, and between 1881 and 1885, the message spread quickly, with an estimated 250,000 people converting to the Christian faith.

By the time of Booth's death in 1912, the Salvation Army had become a family-run ministry, with seven of Booth's children actively holding leadership positions in the organization. Today the Salvation Army serves in more than one hundred countries, sharing the gospel and providing for those in need.

"If there is anything of power
in The Salvation Army today,
it is because God has had all
the adoration of my heart,
all the power of my will, and all
the influence of my life."

WILLIAM BOOTH[4]

DAVID BRAINERD

1718–1747

David Brainerd, the great missionary to the Native Americans in North America, was born in Haddam, Connecticut, in 1718. When Brainerd was nine, his father, a legislator, died, and his mother died five years later. After his parents' deaths he went to live with his aunt until he was eighteen.[1] Brainerd was brought up in the Congregationalist church and made a profession of faith when he was twenty-one. In 1739 he began his studies at Yale College for his ministry degree. During his first year of study, he began to show symptoms of tuberculosis and was forced to leave school due to poor health.

A year later Brainerd returned to school at the height of an evangelical revival under the preaching ministry of George Whitefield. Whitefield, along with others like James Davenport and Gilbert Tennent, had attracted a following of Yale students, and Brainerd was one of them, which caused tension for him on

campus. Yale's leadership was opposed to the evangelical revival happening on campus and was committed to doing what it could to stop it. In 1741 Brainerd commented that a tutor at Yale had "no more grace than a chair."[2] Yale's rector, Thomas Clap, expelled Brainerd for his comment.

Unable to complete his degree, Brainerd was denied ordination. So he shifted his attention to being a missionary and went to work alongside John Sergeant, missionary to the Stockbridge tribe. Brainerd ministered in Massachusetts, New York, Pennsylvania, and New Jersey with remarkable success. He wrote two accounts of the revival happening among the tribes and described his own spiritual journey as he ministered.[3]

Brainerd struggled with depression and poor health throughout his short life but didn't allow his afflictions to prevent him from ministering. In April 1747, weakened by his battle with tuberculosis, Brainerd went to the home of his friend Jonathan Edwards in Northampton, Massachusetts. Later that year on October 9, 1747, Brainerd died at the age of twenty-nine.

Following his death Jonathan Edwards published *An Account of the Life of the Late Reverend Mr. David Brainerd,* which consisted of accounts taken from Brainerd's diaries and was supplemented with Edwards's writing. The book went on to achieve widespread notoriety and continues to encourage missionaries across the globe.

"Nothing grieves me so much as that I cannot live constantly to God's glory."

David Brainerd[4]

LUCY GOODE BROOKS

1818–1900

～～～

Lucy Goode Brooks is the founder of the Friends Asylum for Colored Orphans. Born the daughter of a slave and an unnamed white man, Brooks learned to read during slavery and taught the skill to Albert Royal Brooks—the man who would become her husband in 1839. But in 1858 she and their youngest three children were sold to a man named Daniel Van Groning, who set up a payment plan with Albert for their freedom.[1]

Lucy located three local business owners willing to buy her oldest sons, but a fourth man purchased her oldest daughter, Margaret Ann, and broke his promise to keep her in Richmond, selling the girl to a slave owner in Tennessee.[2] As a result the family was separated, and it took Albert four years to purchase

his wife and three youngest children's freedom back from wages he earned at a tobacco factory. In 1865 their older sons became free when the Union army occupied Richmond, but the family was never reunited with Margaret Ann.

After the Civil War former slaves traveled to Richmond with the hopes of finding lost family members. Having lost a daughter in the slave trade, Lucy was moved by the number of parentless children she saw. She'd been a member of the First Baptist Church of Richmond since 1838 and along with other African Americans in her community had founded the First African Baptist Church in 1841.[3] As an active member of her church community, Lucy was a member of the Ladies Sewing Circle for Charitable Work. She convinced them, along with a local Cedar Creek Meeting of the Society of Friends and several African American churches, that caring for orphans was a worthy mission.

In 1868 the city council in Richmond deeded a portion of land in Jackson Ward to the orphanage, and the Richmond Quaker Society of Friends raised the funds that sponsored the building project. In 1871 the orphanage was completed. Lucy died in 1900, but her legacy continues. Today, the Friends Association for Children, along with three other locations, operates where the orphanage once stood, offering child care, youth support, and family resources for those in need.

"It's amazing what
one woman and her
friends can do."

LUCY GOODE BROOKS[4]

JOHN BUNYAN

1628–1688

⚉∾⚈

John Bunyan, the English author of *The Pilgrim's Progress* and one of the most well-known Christian authors of his time, began married life in his early twenties as a nonbeliever and financially down on his luck. His wife, also with no material wealth to speak of, brought two Puritan books as a dowry to their marriage—and it was those books that planted the seeds for Bunyan's conversion to the Christian faith. Bunyan later recalled overhearing three or four poor women talking about God, and he realized he was missing something. About the same time, he became friends with the minister John Gifford.

Bunyan joined the church and discovered that his newfound faith ushered in a peace he had never experienced. He felt an urgent need to tell other people about his faith in Christ. Bunyan began to preach as a lay minister, and within a few years he was drawing crowds. For twenty years England had enjoyed

the freedom of worship, but that ended with the Restoration of Charles II. Anyone who didn't conform to the Church of England would be arrested. By January 1661 Bunyan was in prison for preaching the gospel. His biggest heartache was being away from his second wife (his first had died) and their four children.

Bunyan could've been set free if he promised not to preach— but he refused. He used his time in prison to write numerous books. He was released from prison for a time when Charles II relented and issued the Declaration of Indulgence.[1] Upon his release he was licensed as a Congregational minister and pastored a church in Bedford. As a pastor Bunyan was again imprisoned for preaching. When he was released the second time, *The Pilgrim's Progress* was published—eventually becoming the bestselling book in history, second only to the Bible.

Bunyan spent the last decade of his life pastoring his church in Bedford and writing and publishing books. In August 1688 he was riding on horseback from Berkshire to London when he caught a cold and fever. He soon died at a friend's home on Snow Hill in Holborn.[2] At the time of his passing, he was one of the most well-known authors in England, and his most successful books were penned in prison.

"I will stay in prison till the
moss grows on my eyelids
rather than disobey God."

JOHN BUNYAN[3]

JOSEPHINE BUTLER

1828–1906

Josephine Butler was among the first to advocate for victims of the sex trade. Born Josephine Elizabeth Grey on April 13, 1828, at the start of the Victorian era in England, she was the fourth daughter of John Grey and his wife, Hannah Annett.[1] Josephine was born into a Christian family and became an avid reader of the Bible. It was her strong faith in God that gave birth to her political activism. While most Victorians believed women were best suited for homemaking and raising children and left social topics to men, Butler's faith compelled her to speak out in support of women being victimized by the sex trade. Butler looked to the Scriptures to make her case. She pointed out that Jesus was compassionate and respectful toward women, which included prostitutes. Her stance beckoned opposition, but she maintained that Jesus' redemptive work was for all people.[2]

In 1869 she started her campaign against the Contagious

Diseases Acts. Law enforcement had been rounding up prostitutes and forcing them to sign a register that publicly linked them to their work forever—making it nearly impossible to leave the sex trade. Even worse, the women were forced to undergo painful exams, and those who were found to be with sexually transmitted diseases were put in jail. Politicians referred to these women as "miserable creatures who were mere masses of rottenness and vehicles of disease" but referred to the men who sought them out as indulging in "natural impulse."[3]

Butler felt compelled by God to speak out against the injustice and double standards of her day. She faced fierce opposition and relentless criticism but felt that if Christ was on her side, that was all she needed. She often said, "God and one woman make a majority."[4] Because of her tireless work, the Contagious Diseases Act was eventually struck down and laws were put in place that prevented young girls from being kidnapped into prostitution. Sadly, Josephine Butler is not a name most people recognize today. It has been said that's because "she didn't champion the right women."[5] Regardless, her work endures as she put in motion efforts that continue to serve women and society today.

"He did not deny me the request of His own heart's love for sinners, and when He makes this revelation He does more; He makes the enquiring soul a partaker of His own heart's love for the world."

Josephine Butler[6]

WILLIAM CAREY

1761–1834

William Carey was a Christian missionary to India. Born in 1761 near Northampton, England, to Edmund and Elizabeth Carey, William was homeschooled by his father until he was fourteen. He took an apprenticeship in a cobbler's shop while teaching himself Greek, Hebrew, Latin, and theology. It was then that a fellow apprentice led him to Christ, and Carey became a Christian.[1]

Carey was frustrated with his fellow Protestants' lack of interest in foreign missions. He argued that Jesus intended for the Great Commission to be for all people in every generation. He said, "Multitudes sit at ease and give themselves no concern about the far greater part of their fellow sinners, who to this day, are lost in ignorance and idolatry."[2]

In 1792 Carey and his family set sail for India. The early years in India were challenging, and the family was financially strained

and frequently ill. Carey caught malaria, and his five-year-old son, Peter, died of dysentery. His wife, Dorothy, struggled with mental health issues—suffering from delusions and even threatening Carey with a knife—and eventually was confined to a room for her safety.

After seven years of struggle, Carey finally experienced a breakthrough. He was invited to relocate near Calcutta, where he would be able to preach legally. Mission finances had increased, and schools were being opened where Carey would teach. Over the next twenty-eight years, Carey and his colaborers translated the Bible into India's major languages and parts of 209 other dialects.[3] Carey campaigned for social reform for widows and orphans. He founded the Serampore College, a divinity school for Indians, which today offers a theological and liberal arts education for 2,500 students.

By the time of Carey's death in 1834, he had served in India for forty-one years. He could point to only seven hundred converts in a nation of millions, but he had planted the seeds for growth and made remarkable progress with Bible translations, social reform, and education.

"Expect great things;
attempt great things."

WILLIAM CAREY[4]

CHARLES COLSON

1931–2012

Charles Colson's life is proof that a man's worst choices don't have to define him. Colson was born during the Great Depression on October 16, 1931, but his parents worked hard so their only child could attend the highly esteemed Buckingham Browne and Nichols School in Cambridge, Massachusetts. Colson was academically gifted and ambitious, earning full scholarships from both Harvard and Brown. Colson chose Brown University and graduated with honors in 1953. The same year he graduated, he was commissioned in the Marine Corps, where he climbed quickly in the ranks, becoming the youngest captain in its history.[1] After his time in the military, he attended George Washington University Law School and graduated in 1959.

Colson was a thirty-eight-year-old lawyer when he joined the Nixon White House. The president quickly saw that Colson was what he described as a "lightning rod," and he was named Nixon's

political point man.[2] Colson's ambition, coupled with his desire to please the president, brought out a dark side that eventually led to his entanglement in the Watergate scandal. Colson was sentenced to prison after he pleaded guilty to obstructing justice.

In the midst of his legal troubles, Colson became a Christian. The sincerity of his faith was questioned and mocked by the media, but ultimately it proved genuine. Colson grew closer to God while in prison and took every opportunity to share his faith with fellow prisoners. When Colson was released he had to decide whether he would return to law and politics or move on to something else.

Colson founded Prison Fellowship Ministries, which became the largest nonprofit prison ministry in the United States, serving inmates and former prisoners, as well as their families. Colson spent his post-prison years advocating for prison reform, ministering to prisoners, and sharing the gospel with those impacted by incarceration. In 1993 Colson received the Templeton Prize for Progress in Religion, and by then he was one of the most influential evangelical voices in the country.

"I found myself increasingly drawn to the idea that God had put me in prison for a purpose and that I should do something for those I had left behind."

CHARLES COLSON[3]

DOROTHY DAY

1897–1980

T oday there are people who long to see Dorothy Day considered for sainthood in the Catholic Church, but in 1941
FBI director J. Edgar Hoover didn't know how to handle her.
Authorities were concerned about her anarchism, and she
was investigated because of her once-communistic views and
numerous arrests for her participation in protests. In 1917 she
went on a hunger strike after being put in jail for protesting in
front of the White House on behalf of women's right to vote.[1]

Born on November 8, 1897, in New York City to journalist
parents, Day experienced what some would describe as a
bohemian youth. She first encountered poverty as a teenager
in Chicago's slums, and her concern for the poor shaped the
trajectory of her life. She was a bright student but dropped out
of college after only two years and went to work as a New York
City journalist writing for numerous socialist and progressive

publications. Her turning point was becoming a devout Catholic at the age of thirty.

Day was heavily influenced by her new faith, and in the years to come she would launch a radical newspaper and open what she referred to as "houses of hospitality" for those in need of food and shelter.[2] Under her leadership Day's Catholic Worker Movement would eventually serve the poor in more than two hundred communities. However, the organization also maintained a political agenda that addressed racial segregation, nuclear warfare, and conflicts abroad while simultaneously opposing abortion, birth control, and the welfare state—which made it challenging to pinpoint her partisan affiliation.

Day wrote several autobiographical works in addition to her writing for the *Catholic Worker*. On November 29, 1980, she died in New York City at Mary House—one of the houses she had established to serve the poor. Her work continues to flourish, with two hundred communities that continue to operate in the United States and twenty-eight more abroad.

"The older I get, the more I meet people, the more convinced I am that we must only work on ourselves, to grow in grace. The only thing we can do about people is to love them."

Dorothy Day[3]

JIM ELLIOT

1927–1956

Jim Elliot lived to be only twenty-eight years old before he was murdered while serving as a missionary to Ecuador, but his life made an impact that is still felt today. Elliot felt called to missionary work while a student at Wheaton College after hearing about a small tribe in Ecuador, and he became convinced it was his life's mission to share the gospel with unreached people. Elliot followed the call to Ecuador, married his schoolmate Elisabeth Howard, and began his ministry serving the Huaorani people (also called the Auca). The Elliots soon had a daughter, Valerie.

The Aucas were an unreached tribe that lived deep in the jungles. In 1955 Elliot and four other missionaries first made contact when missionary Nate Saint dropped supplies and gifts from his plane—a routine they continued for several weeks. In an attempt to begin a friendship, Elliot and his fellow missionaries used a loudspeaker to communicate simple Huaorani phrases

they'd learned, such as *biti miti punimupa*, which means, "I like you, I want to be your friend."[1] The tribesmen appeared to be warming to the men when they reciprocated by giving gifts of their own.

The missionaries located a beach they could stay on, and they were flown in one by one and dropped off. After a couple of days on the beach, a man and woman from the tribe appeared, and the missionaries shared a meal and took the man for a ride in the plane. The exchange was friendly, and they encouraged the tribe members to return with others. On January 8, 1956, tribe members returned—but things didn't go as hoped. Elliot was speared to death along with his four colleagues: Nate Saint, Pete Fleming, Roger Youderian, and Ed McCully. Days later, four of the bodies were identified and one had been washed away.[2] Amazingly, the ministry to the tribe didn't end with their deaths. Elisabeth, Elliot's widow, returned to Ecuador and eventually shared the gospel with the tribe who murdered her husband.

"The will of God is always a
bigger thing than we bargain
for, but we must believe that
whatever it involves, it is good,
acceptable and perfect."

JIM ELLIOT[3]

ESTHER

Fifth century BC

E sther, a Jewish orphan who became the queen of Persia, is the central personality in one of the most well-known stories in the Old Testament. Her story is introduced in the Old Testament book that bears her name. Esther, which means "star" in Persian, was raised by her cousin Mordecai.[1] As a Jewish orphan she was an unlikely candidate to keep company with the king of Persia. But when the king found himself alone and without a wife, a search was launched for a new queen. Esther was one of numerous beautiful women attempting to garner the king's attention, but in addition to being beautiful, Esther had character and spiritual depth that won the king's affection.

After becoming queen, Esther learned that Haman, the king's right-hand man, planned to kill her cousin Mordecai and exterminate the Jews. Mordecai said to her, "If you remain silent at this time, relief and deliverance for the Jews will arise

from another place, but you and your father's family will perish. And who knows but that you have come to your royal position for such a time as this?" (Esther 4:14 NIV). When Esther realized the seriousness of the situation, she decided to save her people even though it meant putting her own life at risk. In Esther's day it was against the law to approach the king without being summoned. It wasn't uncommon for days, weeks, or even months to pass without the queen getting a word with the king. To initiate contact was a serious break in protocol that could easily be interpreted as a sign of disrespect.

After a time of prayer and fasting, Esther stepped forward in faith, knowing that her decision put her in danger and could ultimately require her life. However, the king listened to Esther, and the Jews were saved. Haman's plot was thwarted, and he was hanged in the gallows he'd erected for Mordecai. Today, Jews still celebrate the Feast of Purim as an annual reminder of God's faithfulness to His people.

"Go, gather all the Jews who are present in Shushan, and fast for me; neither eat nor drink for three days, night or day. My maids and I will fast likewise. And so I will go to the king, which is against the law; and if I perish, I perish!" (Esther 4:16 NKJV)

ESTHER

CHARLES FINNEY

1792–1875

Charles Finney—the most well-known revivalist of the Second Great Awakening—was a man who didn't shy away from criticism. As an attorney, theologian, and college president, Finney had formidable communication skills, and he used those skills to make revivals a standard feature of American Christianity.

On a mission to save souls, Finney sought to expand the roles of women in ministry, strengthen local churches, and introduce social reform. He introduced what would be known as "New Measures." This meant praying in a common language that some described as "vulgar" and adopting the "anxious bench"—a Methodist practice in which a bench was placed at the front of the church so people who felt an urgency could contemplate their salvation. During revivals women's prayer gatherings had been a primary way to engage with the community. Finney was criticized for encouraging women to speak at prayer meetings

in the presence of both men and women. Critics called these meetings where women spoke "promiscuous assemblies," but with Finney's support they became common practice for several denominations by the end of the century.[1]

Finney reached the height of his evangelistic ministry in Rochester, New York, between September 10, 1830, and March 6, 1831. During that time he preached ninety-eight sermons. Business owners left signs on their doors telling prospective customers to attend Finney's services. The town's population swelled by two-thirds during the revivals yet crime dropped by two-thirds.[2]

In 1851 he became the president of Oberlin College, where he would serve for fifteen years. Oberlin was the first university to enroll African Americans and women. Finney's time as president of the university allowed him the platform he needed to advocate for social reform—especially the abolition of slavery. He wrote numerous books that instructed thousands of pastors on the best practices of revivals. Despite the criticism he endured, today Finney is regarded by many historians as the father of modern revivalism, and nearly all agree he paved the way for men like Billy Sunday, Dwight Moody, and Billy Graham.

"There must be a waking
up of energy, on the part of
Christians, and an outpouring
of God's Spirit, or the world
will laugh at the church."

CHARLES FINNEY[3]

ELIZABETH FRY

1780–1845

In the early 1800s most people believed that prisons existed to punish rather than rehabilitate inmates. As a result English prisons were known for brutality and inhumanity. Elizabeth Fry, a young wife and mother, prone to anxiety and depression, didn't seem a likely candidate to become England's leading prison reformer.[1]

As a Christ-follower Fry believed it was her responsibility to serve those who were marginalized and forgotten by the rest of society. When she was thirty-three years old, she began to visit the female prisoners at Newgate Prison in London, and she was appalled by the conditions at the prison. On her first visit she saw three hundred women crowded into two rooms with no access to proper hygiene.[2] The women ate, slept, and used the bathroom in the same overcrowded area. Inmates who were mothers kept their children with them in the same horrifying conditions. After her

first visit Fry returned the following day with clean baby clothes, blankets, and supplies. Fry began to visit every day, teaching the women proper hygiene and how to sew so they might earn money upon their release. She read Scripture to the women and gave them Bibles to read on their own.

Prison officials warned Fry she was putting herself at risk for violence and disease, but she disregarded their warnings. Law enforcement officials from surrounding areas began to take note of the positive changes happening at Newgate and started making reforms in their own prisons. In 1818 Fry testified before the House of Commons about the state of England's prison system, paving the way for the Prison Reform Act of 1823.[3]

Fry widened her ministry efforts to women in halfway houses, where she offered access to education and Bible teaching. In 1820 Fry helped open a night shelter in London and organized people who were willing to minister to homeless families. She shared her ideas about prison reform with those in Germany, France, Belgium, and Holland. Up until she died in 1845, she visited and examined the conditions of every ship that carried female prisoners to the British colonies.

"It is an honor to appear on the side of the afflicted."

ELIZABETH FRY[4]

HENRY HIGHLAND GARNET

1815–1882

H enry Highland Garnet was known as one of the leading anti-slavery organizers in the world and a man Cuban patriot José Martí called "America's Moses," but his early years were a struggle.[1] Garnet was born a slave in Maryland, but his parents secured his freedom by fleeing to New York when he was nine years old. During his childhood he suffered an injury that eventually took his leg. Like all free African American families, the Garnets lived in constant danger of being captured by slave catchers.

As a young man in his twenties, Garnet proved to be a compelling speaker. He married Julia Ward Williams, a teacher, in 1841, and Garnet began to pursue his calling as a minister and an abolitionist. In 1843 he delivered a speech at the National Negro

Convention urging slaves to rise up against their slave masters and secure their freedom—an unconventional and highly criticized approach for the time. In 1864 Garnet was named the pastor of the Fifteenth Street Presbyterian Church in Washington, DC. The following year he preached a sermon to the United States Congress, becoming the first African American to do so.

Garnet felt disappointment as the Civil War came to a close because he thought it was a premature celebration of the end of slavery. Nevertheless, Garnet encouraged abolitionists to continue fighting and refresh their efforts by confronting slavery in Cuba and Brazil. In 1872 he organized the Cuban Anti-Slavery Committee, which opened branches in numerous states in the United States. Garnet grew more devout in his faith and active in eradicating slavery at home and abroad. In 1881 President James Garfield appointed Garnet as ambassador to Liberia, but he died two months after his arrival.

"If slavery has been destroyed merely from necessity, let every class be enfranchised at the dictation of justice. Then we shall have a Constitution that shall be reverenced by all . . . and a Union that shall be . . . loved by a . . . patriotic people, and which can never be severed."

HENRY HIGHLAND GARNET[2]

GEORGE FRIDERIC HANDEL

1685–1759

George Frideric Handel is celebrated today as one of the world's most prestigious musicians and composers. But during the years he was creating music, his world was filled with criticism and uncertainty. Handel was born in Germany in February 1685, and his father planned for him to study law, but Handel showed an early aptitude for music. However, his father was against Handel's musical aspirations and forbade him to play. Nevertheless, young Handel somehow got his hands on a small clavichord and sneaked around to practice the instrument. When Handel was eight he shocked his family at church one Sunday when he climbed on the organ bench and played the postlude.[1]

Handel enrolled in law school but soon left his studies to

pursue music. He traveled to different cities, learning what he could about various styles of music, and in 1711 the twenty-six-year-old settled in London. His operas enjoyed wide acceptance there, making him an established member of the English music scene.

In the 1730s Handel was struggling financially, and in an attempt to keep his creditors paid, he was composing up to four operas per year. The heavy workload took its toll on his body, and he suffered a stroke that paralyzed his right arm. Doctors believed he would live but that his days as a musician were over. But Handel refused to accept his prognosis, and his miraculous recovery stunned everyone.

In 1741 Handel was deep in debt and no longer the "it" composer. Poet Charles Jennens sent Handel a libretto, and Handel used Scripture references and told the life of Jesus Christ through the libretto. Over just twenty-three days, Handel composed a 260-page oratorio that he titled *Messiah*. Despite his heavy debt, Handel insisted all proceeds be given to widows and orphans. It opened to rave reviews and exceeded financial expectations.

Forty years later an English musicologist wrote, "This great work has been heard in all parts of the kingdom with increasing reverence and delight; it has fed the hungry, clothed the naked, fostered the orphan and enriched succeeding managers of the oratorios, more than any single production in this or any other country."[2]

"I have myself been a very
sick man, and am now
cured; I was a prisoner
and have been set free."

George Frideric Handel[3]

MAHALIA JACKSON

1911–1972

Mahalia Jackson is known as the "Queen of Gospel Singers" and the "Voice of the Civil Rights Movement," but her rise to the top began in hardship. Born in New Orleans on October 26, 1911, she entered into a world of poverty. Her mother died when Mahalia was six, and she was sent to live with her aunt. Constant financial strain forced her to leave school in the eighth grade to find work as a cook and a laundry worker.

At sixteen Jackson moved to Chicago, where she would gain notoriety in the choir at the Greater Salem Baptist Church.[1] Jackson's music was influenced by Bessie Smith and other blues singers, which sometimes put her at odds with traditional gospel music purists. Critics complained that she was singing the blues, and some ministers didn't want that in their churches. Louis Armstrong and Duke Ellington tried to convince Jackson to record jazz, but Jackson refused because her faith was at the core

of who she was. She told Ellington, "Duke, my music is the music of the Lord."[2] Despite the criticism Jackson was determined her music would reflect her faith and artistic vision.

In her early career she traveled widely, performed for European royalty, and played Carnegie Hall on five occasions. In 1960 she was invited to sing the national anthem at John F. Kennedy's inauguration. Already a famous gospel singer, Jackson gained more renown during the civil rights movement as she was a close friend and confidant of the Reverend Martin Luther King Jr. Her voice was known as the soundtrack for the civil rights movement. She performed at Selma, at the March on Washington, and for Dr. King's funeral.[3]

Later in life, despite failing health, Jackson continued to perform and travel extensively. She died of heart failure in a suburb of Chicago on January 27, 1972; she was sixty years old. She'd confronted poverty, criticism, and racism, and in the process she became the voice of a generation.

"I have hopes that my singing
will break down some
of the hate and fear that
divide the white and black
people in this country."

MAHALIA JACKSON[4]

JOAN OF ARC

circa 1412–1431

Joan of Arc believed it was God's will for her to lead France to victory in the long-standing war with England. When the peasant girl was about thirteen, she was working in her father's garden when she heard a voice instructing her to lead a virtuous life. These episodes came with more frequency, and she later heard a voice telling her she was to assist the dauphin, who was France's rightful heir, in getting crowned.[1]

With the help of a cousin, she got an audience with Robert de Baudricourt, the local lord, to tell him of her plans, but he dismissed her and sent her home. Nine months later, she tried again with the dauphin, Charles, and told him her hopes. He turned her over to the churchmen from the University of Poitiers, and she was questioned for weeks and found to be of noble character. Soon, she found herself alongside four thousand troops as they assisted the besieged city of Orléans.

Although she wasn't a commander, Joan played a formidable role as she led troops in winning back several forts that surrounded Orléans. She was wounded when she took an arrow in the shoulder during the battle for the fort of Les Tourelles, but she recovered and quickly returned to battle. Soon the French reoccupied the city of Orléans. A few months later, with more territory recaptured, the dauphin was crowned the king of France. But suddenly the newly crowned king lost his nerve, and Joan's requests to drive the English out of Paris went unanswered.

The following year, eighteen-year-old Joan was captured by the English and put in prison for five months. She was questioned repeatedly and charged on seventy counts of heresy. Officials were troubled that she claimed to hear the voice of God, and they sentenced her to death. On May 30, 1431, Joan walked to the public square to be burned at the stake. She knelt and prayed for her enemies. As the flames drew close to her skin, Joan asked for a cross to be held near her. As she gazed at the cross, her last word was "Jesus." Twenty-five years later, she was declared innocent. In 1920 she was canonized as a saint by the Roman Catholic Church.

"If I were to say that God sent
me, I shall be condemned,
but God really did send me."

JOAN OF ARC[2]

ABSALOM JONES

1746–1818

~~~~~~~~~~

Absalom Jones was the first African American priest ordained in the Episcopal Church. Jones was born into slavery in 1746, and his family worked the fields of a wealthy land-owner, Abraham Wynkoop.[1] When Jones was a child, Wynkoop recognized his aptitude and intelligence and ordered that he work in the house, where he learned to read and saved up to buy books.

After Wynkoop's death, the landowner's son Benjamin sold the plantation along with Jones's mother and six siblings. Benjamin opened a store in Philadelphia, and he brought Jones with him to work the store. At night Jones attended a school run by Quakers for African Americans.

When Jones was twenty he married Mary Thomas, who was enslaved to a fellow member of Benjamin's church. Jones, along with his father-in-law, repeatedly attempted to purchase her freedom as well as his own. Finally, he secured his wife's freedom,

but it would be six more years until he secured his own.[2] At last, in 1784 Jones was freed from slavery, and he began attending worship services at St. George's Methodist Episcopal Church. He met Richard Allen, and the two became lifelong friends, eventually opening the Free African Society, an organization committed to helping freed slaves in Philadelphia.[3]

The Free African Society held worship services that would become the African Church of Philadelphia. Jones felt called to pastoral ministry, and he was ordained as a deacon in 1795. In 1802 he became the first African American priest. His ordination was groundbreaking, but his struggles with racial inequality were far from over. Now he had all the responsibilities of shepherding a congregation but wasn't allowed to sit with white clergy at conventions or mingle with fellow clergy members. People were hesitant about the idea of an African American priest, and he was continually confronted with resistance from the general public.

But for Jones faith and freedom went hand in hand. Jones's efforts extended outside the church walls and reached into the public square. In 1797 Jones participated in presenting the Fugitive Slave Act. Even with the progress he'd made and the contributions he'd offered, he continued to work for abolitionist causes until his death in 1818.

"To arise out of the dust and shake ourselves, and throw off that servile fear, that the habit of oppression and bondage trained us up in. And in meekness and fear, we would desire to walk in the liberty wherewith Christ has made us free."

ABSALOM JONES[4]

ADONIRAM JUDSON

1788–1850

❧～❧

Adoniram Judson is known as the first American missionary, but he began college as an unbeliever. Judson was raised in a devout home as the son of a Congregationalist pastor. Still, while attending Brown University, he grew skeptical about his faith, and the untimely death of a close friend left him unsettled. So even though he wasn't yet a Christian, his curiosity compelled him to enroll at Andover Seminary in Massachusetts, and it was there he became a follower of Jesus Christ and answered a call to foreign missions.[1]

Over two weeks in February 1812, Judson was ordained to the gospel ministry and married Ann Hasseltine. He and his new wife, along with another couple, set sail for Calcutta, India—becoming the first Americans to move to another country for the sake of gospel ministry.[2]

India was opposed to Judson's presence, and the missionaries

were soon forced to leave the country. Judson shifted his focus and would dedicate forty years of his life to serving in Burma, the nation now known as Myanmar. The family was frequently ill, and three of their children died. Judson's wife became so sick she had to return to America for two years to recover.

In 1824 all Western men were presumed spies by the Burmese emperor, and he had them put in prison, including Judson. He spent twenty-one months imprisoned on false charges in a prison described as "too vile to house animals."[3] Judson was tortured in prison and sometimes spent all night with his feet shackled and suspended, so only his head and shoulders reached the ground. Finally, he was released to serve as a translator in the peace negotiations between Burma and England, but Judson's struggles were far from over. In 1826 his wife died, and his two-year-old daughter died six months later.

In 1830 Judson emerged from seclusion with a new resolve to share the gospel. During his forty-year ministry, he led hundreds of Burmese people to Christ, translated the Bible and other Christian literature into two languages, wrote several discipleship tracts, and motivated Baptists in America to unify for the sake of gospel missions. In 2014 a census was taken that revealed there are more than three million believers in Myanmar today.[4]

"If I had not felt certain that
every additional trial was
ordered by infinite love and
mercy, I could not have survived
my accumulated suffering."

ADONIRAM JUDSON[5]

ANN HASSELTINE JUDSON

1789–1826

$\sim\!\!\sim\!\!\sim$

Ann Hasseltine Judson was the first female missionary to be sent to foreign soil. Ann, known as "Nancy," was born in December 1789 in Bradford, Massachusetts. The youngest of five children, she and her family attended the Congregationalist church, but religion factored little into the young woman's life.

Growing up during the Second Great Awakening, Ann heard the gospel but struggled with coming to terms with her faith. During a time of spiritual uncertainty, she had a conversation with a godly aunt who helped her understand the Christian faith. In 1806 Ann and her family attended a revival, and she made a public confession of her faith in Christ, as did the rest of the family.[1]

In June 1810 Adoniram Judson and three others who had committed to living as missionaries came to lunch at the Hasseltine home. In July Judson wrote Ann's father a letter asking permission to marry his daughter and take her overseas to the mission field. Ann's father left the decision up to her, and Ann believed it to be God's will for her life.[2] They were married on February 5, 1812, and set sail for India, but within ten days of their arrival they were forced to leave the country.

Ultimately, the couple arrived in Burma, where they would begin a forty-year ministry. They learned the language and shared the gospel with the Burmese people, but missionary life was difficult. In 1821 Ann was suffering from liver problems and returned to America for medical care. Shortly after her return to Burma, her husband and several other Westerners were imprisoned on false charges of espionage. The prison conditions were horrific, and Adoniram was brutally tortured. Ann saved his life by taking daily food portions to the prison, advocating for him with the government, and pleading with officials for his life. Because of her advocacy he was released in 1826, but Ann soon fell ill. She died on October 24, 1826. The last words she spoke were in Burmese, the language of the people she'd grown to love and offer her life in service to as an act of faith.[3]

"I began to discover a beauty in the way of salvation by Christ. He appeared to be just such a Savior as I needed. I saw how God could be just, saving sinners through him. I committed my soul into his hands."

ANN HASSELTINE JUDSON[4]

CORETTA SCOTT KING

1927–2006

~~~~~~~~

Coretta Scott King was one of the most influential women in the civil rights movement. Born in Marion, Alabama, she graduated as valedictorian from her class at Lincoln High School. She earned a bachelor's degree in music and then went on to earn additional degrees in voice and violin from Boston's New England Conservatory of Music.[1] As a student in Boston, she met Martin Luther King Jr., who was studying for his doctorate at Boston University. They married on June 18, 1953, and later that year moved to Montgomery, Alabama, where Coretta took on the responsibilities of a pastor's wife as Dr. King ministered at Dexter Avenue Baptist Church.

Between 1955 and 1963, the couple had four children together,

and Coretta balanced motherhood and her role as a social justice advocate. As the civil rights movement progressed, Dexter Avenue Baptist Church became a focal point for the movement. Unfortunately, because of their leadership the King home was often the target of violence from white supremacist groups, and she lived with ongoing threats to their safety.

After Dr. King's assassination in Memphis on April 4, 1968, Coretta devoted her focus and commitment to building programs for the Martin Luther King, Jr. Center for Nonviolent Social Change in Atlanta. As a lifelong advocate of interracial coalitions, she tirelessly communicated the message of nonviolence across every corner of the world. She met with heads of state, spiritual leaders, and local organizers of the civil rights movement.

As one of the most notable leaders of her time, she was honored with more than sixty honorary doctorate degrees. In addition, she wrote three books, authored a nationally syndicated newspaper column, and championed dozens of organizations committed to social justice. She died in 2006, and thousands stood in line at Ebenezer Baptist Church in Atlanta to pay their respects.

"I always felt that what was happening in Montgomery was part of God's will and purpose, and we were put there to be in the forefront of that struggle, and it wasn't just a struggle relegated to Montgomery, Alabama or the South, but that it had worldwide implications."

CORETTA SCOTT KING[2]

PHOEBE KNAPP

1839–1908

⁓⁓⁓

P hoebe Knapp was a prominent writer who composed more than five hundred gospel songs. Knapp was born on March 9, 1839, to New York City physician Walter Palmer and his wife, Phoebe—whom young Phoebe was named after. The Palmers raised Phoebe in a Christian home that was known as a place of song and prayer. When she was only sixteen, Phoebe married Joseph Knapp, who founded the Metropolitan Life Insurance Company and was a well-known Sunday school worker. The couple worshiped at the John Street Methodist Church in New York City, where Fanny Crosby attended.[1]

Knapp enjoyed a prosperous lifestyle; she wore lavish gowns and entertained the most prominent people of the day in the family mansion in Brooklyn. But as a Christian Knapp's faith compelled her to serve the poor and bring reform to the community. As a result she donated large amounts of money to the poor

and enlisted social and government leaders who supported her causes.

Knapp was also drawn to music. After her husband's death she was left a large sum of money, most of which she gave to charity. In 1898 she moved into a suite at the Savoy Hotel in New York City and had an organ put in her room. She wrote more than five hundred hymns, including "Blessed Assurance," which she wrote with her friend Fanny Crosby. As the story goes Knapp had written a melody and felt a sense of urgency about what she'd composed. She went to Crosby's home and played her what she'd written. Later, Crosby said, "My friend, Mrs. Knapp, composed a melody and played it over to me two or three times on the piano. She then asked me what it said, and I immediately replied, 'Blessed Assurance, Jesus is mine! O what a foretaste of glory divine!'"[2] In just a few minutes, the duo had finished writing the song that would come to be known as a gospel standard.

Blessed assurance, Jesus is mine

Oh, what a foretaste of glory divine

Heir of salvation, purchase of God

Born of His spirit, washed in His blood.

PHOEBE KNAPP

JOHN LEWIS

1940–2020

ᕙᕗᕤᕤᕗᕙ

Congressman John Lewis was called the "Conscience of Congress" and was known as one of the "Big Six" leaders in the civil rights movement. Lewis rose to national prominence during his decades of service as a human rights activist. Born on February 21, 1940, to sharecropper parents in Troy, Alabama, he was disappointed in 1954 when the Supreme Court's ruling on *Brown v. the Board of Education* didn't impact his school experience. For the most part schools in the South remained segregated. But as a young man, Lewis was motivated by Dr. Martin Luther King Jr.'s sermons to commit himself to a life of public service to bring about social reform.[1]

Lewis said of Dr. King, "He was not concerned about the streets of heaven and the pearly gates and the streets paved with milk and honey. He was more concerned about the streets of Montgomery and the way that Black people and poor people were

being treated in Montgomery."[2] In 1957 Lewis enrolled at the American Baptist Theological Seminary in Nashville, and faith remained the driving force that carried him through the turmoil to come.

Lewis organized demonstrations against segregated restaurants, bathrooms, hotels, public parks, and swimming pools. In 1961 he was one of the original thirteen Freedom Riders who challenged the segregated interstate system in the South. On March 7, 1965, Lewis was injured when a trooper cracked his skull with a club during a partial march across the Edmund Pettus Bridge in Selma, Alabama. That date came to be known as Bloody Sunday.[3] Televised footage of the beatings led to support for the Voting Rights Act, which Lyndon B. Johnson passed eight days later.

Between 1960 and 1966, Lewis was arrested forty times and beaten bloody on numerous occasions. During the 1961 Freedom Rides, he was left in a pool of his own blood outside a Greyhound bus station after he and numerous others were beaten by a crowd of hundreds of white people. Change was slow, but Lewis believed transformation started at the local level. In 1981 Lewis was elected to Atlanta's city council. He was elected to Congress in November 1986 and served until his death in 2020.

"Do not get lost in a sea of despair. Be hopeful, be optimistic. Our struggle is not the struggle of a day, a week, a month, or a year, it is the struggle of a lifetime. Never, ever be afraid to make some noise and get in good trouble, necessary trouble."

JOHN LEWIS[4]

MARY LYON

1797–1849

⌍⌌⌍⌌⌍⌌

In 1837 Mary Lyon founded Mount Holyoke Female Seminary nearly one hundred years before women gained the right to vote. During that era there were 120 colleges available to men, but none for women.[1] Born in Buckland, Massachusetts, on February 28, 1797, Lyon began teaching when she was seventeen to earn money to pay for her education. Private academies, often called seminaries, were opening in New England, but Lyon came from a family of modest means and couldn't afford the tuition. To complicate matters, the course of study offered to women was less rigorous than education available to men, and the curriculum was often reduced to subjects like needlework and drawing.

From 1817 to 1821, Lyon pursued her education. After finishing school she took a job teaching for three years and opened a school in her hometown. She then took a teaching position at Ipswich Female Seminary, where she taught for the next six years. In 1834

Lyon knew she had to improve the educational opportunities for women in America. A devout Christian, she believed educational opportunities should be available to all people regardless of gender or economic status.[2] She left her role at Ipswich to begin fundraising. Mindful of her own struggles and aware that countless women were facing similar dilemmas, she sought to open educational institutions for women that were both academically challenging and affordable.

At the time the United States was heavily impacted by economic depression, and Lyon faced considerable challenges raising the money, but she persisted, and her effort paid off. On November 8, 1837, the Mount Holyoke Female Seminary opened its doors. Eighty students were admitted after passing a challenging oral exam that covered English, grammar, math, US history, and geography. The following year two hundred women applied, and ninety were accepted. The school set high standards for graduation, requiring seven courses in math and science—a bar set far higher than other female seminaries. In 1861 the curriculum expanded from three years to four, and in 1893 the school was renamed Mount Holyoke College. To date the school has educated more than thirty-three thousand women, including Emily Dickinson. Graduates have made significant contributions in the fields of science, medicine, law, government, and the arts.

"There is nothing in the universe that I fear, but that I shall not know all my duty, or shall fail to do it."

Mary Lyon[3]

NELSON MANDELA

1918–2013

Nelson Mandela was an international icon who served as South Africa's first black president from 1994 to 1999. He was a social rights activist, philanthropist, and politician. For more than twenty years, Mandela ran a nonviolent and peaceful campaign against the South African government to confront racist policies.

He was born on July 18, 1918, and given the name Rolihlahla Mandela in the small village of Mvezo, which sat on the banks of the Mbashe River in Transkei, South Africa. Mandela took pleasure in pointing out that his birth name translated as "troublemaker." When he was seven years old, he received his more common English name from a teacher.

Mandela was forty-four years old when he was charged with sabotage and conspiracy to overthrow the state—both capital crimes. He was shackled and put on a ferry to Robben Island Prison. He wouldn't be released until he was seventy-one.

Robben Island is surrounded by shark-infested waters seven miles off the coast of Cape Town. His time in prison was characterized by isolation, malicious guards, and boredom. Mandela was revered among his fellow prisoners, causing him to be singled out by guards and forcing him to take the brunt of the cruel acts. However, Mandela used his time in prison to learn, and he credited his imprisonment for teaching him strategies that would make him the future president.

In 1993 Mandela won the Nobel Peace Prize, and the following year he was elected as the president of South Africa. He was the first South African politician elected in a fully democratic election. These achievements came after spending twenty-seven years in prison for his work to end apartheid. When asked how he kept his feelings in check when he'd been confronted with such horrendous treatment, he answered, "Hating clouds the mind. It gets in the way of strategy. Leaders cannot afford to hate."[1]

"I have fought against white domination, and I have fought against black domination. I have cherished the ideal of a democratic and free society. . . . It is an ideal . . . which I hope to . . . see realized. But my lord, if it needs be, it is an ideal for which I am prepared to die."

NELSON MANDELA[2]

JUSTIN MARTYR

circa 100–circa 165

❧

Justin Martyr was an evangelist, apologist, and philosopher who spent his life discerning truth from error. He was so confident in his faith that when he was arrested in Rome and asked to denounce his religious beliefs, he replied, "No one who is rightly minded turns from true belief to false."[1]

Born to pagan parents in the Roman city of Flavia Neapolis, Justin began his early years searching for the meaning of life in modern philosophy, but he came up empty-handed. Then, around AD 130, he spoke with an elderly man about Christianity, and it was a conversation that changed the trajectory of his life. He later said, "A fire was suddenly kindled in my soul. I fell in love with the prophets and these men who had loved Christ; I reflected on all their words and found that this philosophy alone was true and profitable. This is how and why I became a philosopher. And I wish that everyone felt the same way I do."[2]

After his conversion to Christianity, Justin continued as a philosopher with a new focus on reconciling faith and reason. His teaching took him to Ephesus and Rome. In Rome he opened a Christian school and wrote about faith. Justin's *First Apology*, published in 155, sought to discuss the Christian faith and addressed Emperor Antoninus Pius. In it he explained that Christianity wasn't a threat to the state and should be a legal religion. It also gained notoriety for its description of early Christian worship.

In 161 Justin's *Second Apology* was published when Marcus Aurelius became emperor. Justin wrote to prove that the Christian faith alone was truly rational. Four years later Justin's beliefs would be put to the test when he and his followers were arrested for their faith. Soon after, Justin was beheaded, and he was surnamed Martyr.

"If we are punished for the
sake of our Lord Jesus Christ,
we hope to be saved."

JUSTIN MARTYR[3]

MARY, MOTHER OF JESUS

First century

Mary, the mother of Jesus, is arguably the most well-known woman in the Bible. In Mary's day, the customary age for a betrothal was thirteen to fourteen, so she was likely around that age when their families arranged her engagement to Joseph. Not long after their engagement, the angel Gabriel appeared to Mary and told her she would carry the long-awaited Messiah and give birth to the Savior of the world (Luke 1:31–32).

This scenario presented a dilemma for Mary. The question arose, How could she give birth to the Christ-child if she'd never been intimate with a man? "And Mary said to the angel, 'How will this be, since I am a virgin?'" (v. 34). Gabriel responded to Mary's question, saying that the "Holy One who is to be born will

be called the Son of God" (v. 35 NKJV). She was satisfied with his answer and said, "Behold, I am the servant of the Lord; let it be to me according to your word" (v. 38).

By all accounts Mary was an ordinary young woman with extraordinary faith. Despite the risks, she was committed to obeying God and leaving the consequences of her obedience to Him. God was gracious to Mary and honored her obedience. She and Joseph married, and Mary indeed gave birth to the Christ-child. However, Mary's life wasn't without hardship. History suggests Joseph died and left Mary a widow, and the day would come when she would watch Jesus suffer and die on a cross.

Mary's life demonstrates that people of faith don't have to understand how everything will work out before they step out in obedience. And Mary could say, "For he who is mighty has done great things for me, and holy is his name" (Luke 1:49).

"Behold, I am the servant of the Lord; let it be to me according to your word"

MARY, MOTHER OF JESUS[1]

WANG MING-DAO

1900–1991

～～✦～～

Wang Ming-Dao is known as one of the most influential and respected Chinese Christians in history. Born in 1900 in Beijing, Ming-Dao experienced poverty and frequent sickness early in life. Nevertheless, he became a Christian at fourteen and in 1919 began his ministry as a teacher at a Presbyterian school in Baoding. Early in his ministry Ming-Dao showed a willingness to hold fast to his beliefs, regardless of the consequences, when he became convinced that the Bible taught baptism by immersion.[1] His colleagues at the Presbyterian school where he taught attempted to convince him otherwise, warning he would lose his job if he didn't align his teaching with their doctrine. Ming-Dao refused to back down and ultimately was fired from his teaching post.

In 1923 Ming-Dao began preaching the convention circuit and evangelistic campaigns. Then, in 1937 Beijing fell to Japanese forces in the Second Sino-Japanese War. Two years later the

Japanese Ministry of Education forced all magazines and newspapers to publish propaganda supporting the Japanese military. Ming-Dao had been a writer for the *Spiritual Food Quarterly* for more than ten years when he was given the ultimatum to be used as a political mouthpiece or close the doors of the publishing house.[2] He continued to publish without writing supporting comments about the government.

Later, during the rise of communism, the Three-Self Patriotic Movement was introduced, which sought to link Chinese Christians to Chinese nationalism. Ming-Dao opposed the movement on the basis of his faith and wrote about his refusal to participate. On August 7, 1955, he and his wife and other church members were arrested for being counter-revolutionary. He received a long sentence but served only one year after confessing to crimes he didn't commit. One of the terms of his release was that he had to join the Three-Self Church and preach as a part of that movement. Ming-Dao was fearful for his wife and himself and wanted to avoid a lengthy prison sentence. He had a decision to make: go along with the government's demands and avoid prison, or stand for his faith and be imprisoned. He chose the latter. On April 29, 1957, Ming-Dao and his wife were arrested a second time. Ming-Dao served twenty-two years in prison while experiencing poor health and mistreatment from fellow inmates. In 1979 he was released from prison and rejoined his wife, who had been released in 1974.[3]

"Our first concern is to manifest the Lord in our lives, to conduct ourselves so that whenever people watch us they will see how they should live."

WANG MING-DAO[4]

HANNAH MORE

1745–1833

～～～

Hannah More was left at the altar three times—by the same man. The only bright side to her public humiliation was that the untrustworthy groom compensated More with a lifetime annuity of two hundred pounds, which was enough to secure her financial independence.[1] More's father, Jacob, was a rarity in his day and believed women should be educated. He saw to it that his five daughters, including his fourth-born, Hannah, received a quality education.

More began writing her first plays while studying at the boarding school in which she would later teach. It was there she met David Garrick, an actor and manager who would play a crucial role in her success as a playwright. In the coming years, she would enjoy critical success for plays such as *The Inflexible Captive* and *Percy*.

More was uncomfortable about her status as a well-known

playwright and woman of society. Her writing centered on moral, Christian themes, and she viewed herself as a hypocrite because the way she lived didn't align with the characters she created. She began to realize theater wasn't the best outlet for her creativity and she would need another avenue to convey godliness.

After hearing several sermons preached by John Newton, she felt inspired to use her writing as a platform to educate London's aristocrats in the foundations of Scripture and to encourage them to act on their faith. As a result she wrote *Sacred Dramas,* a series of skits dramatizing Scripture. It was a risky move considering other writers had received severe criticism for similar pursuits. But More was convinced that society's elite needed to understand the Bible. She believed that reform needed to start at the top and trickle down to influence lower classes. More knew biblical illiteracy was rampant among aristocrats, so in October 1789, she and her sister Martha opened their first Sunday school. The local farmers claimed, "religion would be the ruin of agriculture."[2] But More was not discouraged by her critics. Within ten years, they would open more than a dozen schools in neighboring villages. Throughout her life More advocated to advance education and opportunities for the poor. She died on September 7, 1833.

"Obstacles are those frightful
things you see when you take
your eyes off the goal."

HANNAH MORE

LUCRETIA MOTT

1793–1880

Lucretia Mott was a woman of small stature and huge ambition. Despite being just under five feet tall and less than one hundred pounds, Mott was a formidable presence.[1] The early abolitionist and social reformer who helped start the women's rights movement was a Quaker, and her faith inspired her to believe that all people are equal under God. Mott dedicated her life to speaking up on behalf of African Americans, women, and other marginalized groups.

Born on January 3, 1793, in Nantucket, Massachusetts, Lucretia was the second of five children born to Thomas Coffin and Ann Folger. Her parents were devout Christians who lived out their beliefs in the home. She attended a Quaker boarding school and excelled in her coursework. She met her future husband, James Mott, when she was a teenager, and her studies led her to teach.

However, as an educator Mott was frustrated by the inequality she witnessed between male and female teachers.

In 1809 Mott's family moved to Philadelphia, and James relocated with them. Two years later, the couple married and eventually had six children. James was passionate about social reform and supported his wife's role as an abolitionist. In the 1830s it was dangerous to participate in the anti-slavery movement, and abolitionists were often the target of mob violence, but Mott was unmoved. In 1833 she launched the Philadelphia Anti-Slavery Society. In 1838 she hosted the second Anti-Slavery Convention of American Women in Philadelphia, bringing together 175 abolitionists, both Black and White, from ten states.[2] Angered by the interaction between races, seventeen thousand protestors gathered outside the hall and threatened the abolitionists' lives. The women escaped without harm, but protestors burned down the building and then attempted to set Mott's home on fire.

Despite continual threats Mott continued her work. In 1848 she and Elizabeth Cady Stanton founded a Women's Rights Convention in Seneca, New York, attended by Frederick Douglass. Mott believed the anti-slavery movement and women's rights were interconnected, and she continued to fight for both causes. In 1864 Mott and her husband, along with other Quakers, founded Swarthmore College, a leading liberal arts college. Mott died in Philadelphia on November 11, 1880, at age eighty-seven.[3]

"Any great change must expect opposition, because it shakes the very foundation of privilege."

LUCRETIA MOTT[4]

WATCHMAN NEE

1903–1972

Watchman Nee is the most well-known Chinese Christian pastor in history. He was born in 1903 in Foochow, China. Starting at an early age, Nee excelled in his studies and ranked first in his class. When he was seventeen, he became a Christian. He later said, "From the evening I was saved, I began to live a new life, for the life of the eternal God had entered into me."[1] Nee didn't attend seminary but dedicated himself to a lifetime of study. Early in his ministry he got in the habit of spending a third of his income on Christian books and acquired a collection of more than three thousand titles.

Nee was the grandson of a Congregational minister, and his mother had been raised Methodist. Nee was converted by evangelist preacher Dora Yo and was grateful that missionaries had brought the gospel to China. But he also criticized their approach and found local churches to be superficial, complaining that

converts seldom grew to spiritual maturity. In 1922 Nee formed an independent Christian assembly in Foochow that practiced a weekly Lord's Supper and believer's baptism. Rather than being governed by a pastor, oversight came from a board of elders. In 1928 he moved his base to Shanghai, and outsiders named them "Little Flock Church."[2] By 1950 they had grown to seventy thousand members in seven hundred assemblies.

Throughout his ministry Nee suffered from a variety of health problems, including tuberculosis. In 1934 he married Charity Chang. In March 1952, after the communist takeover of China, Nee was arrested for preaching the gospel. He was wrongly condemned and in 1956 was sentenced to fifteen years in prison. Nee wouldn't see freedom again; he died in prison on May 30, 1972. Despite Nee's suffering, four hundred churches had been planted in China by the time of his arrest. His books continue to be widely read and are contained in a set of sixty-two volumes, *The Collected Works of Watchman Nee*, which range from his first publication in 1922 to his last speaking engagement in 1950.[3]

"God makes it quite clear in
His Word that He has only
one answer to every human
need—His Son, Jesus Christ."

Watchman Nee[4]

FLANNERY O'CONNOR

1925–1964

F lannery O'Connor is known as one of the most prolific short story writers of the twentieth century. Her writing was heavily influenced by her Roman Catholic faith and being raised in the South. Born Mary Flannery O'Connor on March 25, 1925, in Savannah, Georgia, to parents Edward O'Connor and Regina Cline, she was immersed in Catholic culture from birth. It was often said she was "conceived in the shadow of the cathedral."[1]

O'Connor's education began in Savannah's parochial schools. When she was thirteen, the family moved to Milledgeville, Georgia, due to her father's poor health. Two years later, her father died of lupus. Her father's death would mark her writing with a dominant presence of widows and orphans in her stories.[2]

As a college student O'Connor studied at the elite Iowa Writers' Workshop, and it was then that she started keeping a handwritten diary and sought to deepen her prayer life. In one entry she prayed, "Dear God, I am so discouraged about my work . . . Please help me dear God get something else accepted. That is so far from what I deserve, of course, that I am naturally struck with the nerve of it."[3]

O'Connor did become widely published. Her publications include two novels, *Wise Blood* and *The Violent Bear It Away*, and a widely celebrated collection of short stories, including *A Good Man Is Hard to Find and Other Stories, Everything That Rises Must Converge*, and *The Complete Stories.*

O'Connor's work depicted dark humor with a sharp sense of southern dialect and a keen sense of irony. Some critics viewed O'Connor's work as unladylike for the era. Still, despite the criticism, O'Connor believed her job as a writer was to convey reality, no matter how difficult it was to accept.

In 1950 on a train ride from Connecticut to Georgia, O'Connor was afflicted with her first attack of lupus—the same disease that killed her father and would ultimately take her life at the age of thirty-nine.[4] For the next thirteen years, O'Connor suffered from poor health. But it was during those years of suffering that her most prolific writing was done, and she produced some of the greatest stories in American literature. And it was during those years of suffering that the prayers she recorded in her journal were answered.

"Dear Lord please make me want You. It would be the greatest bliss. Not just to want You when I think about You but to want You all the time, to think about You all the time, to have it like a cancer in me."

FLANNERY O'CONNOR[5]

RAHAB

circa 1400 BC

Rahab was an ancestor of Jesus and a prostitute introduced in the Old Testament book of Joshua. She lived in the city of Jericho and owned a home that was positioned snugly in the thick surrounding walls of the city. As a Canaanite, Rahab descended from a people group disliked by the Israelites. Moses, the leader of the Israelites, died, and Joshua was named his successor. Forty years earlier, as chronicled in Numbers 13, Joshua and Caleb had traveled to Jericho to spy out the land. They returned to the Israelites and pleaded with them to take possession of the land of promise, but they didn't succeed in convincing them. This time the Israelites would take the land, and Joshua sent two spies ahead to ensure that happened. The spies went to Rahab's home, and she hid them. Later, Rahab was questioned by the king of Jericho and asked if she knew where the spies were.

"And she said, 'True, the men came to me, but I did not know

where they were from. And when the gate was about to be closed at dark, the men went out. I do not know where the men went. Pursue them quickly, for you will overtake them.' But she had brought them up to the roof and hid them with the stalks of flax that she had laid in order on the roof" (Joshua 2:4–6).

After the king left, Rahab struck a deal with the spies and asked them to protect her family. Rahab knew God had parted the Red Sea on behalf of the Israelites, and she had faith He would continue to protect them (Joshua 2:12–14).

Rahab's story demonstrates that God's grace is without boundaries. Rahab was a prostitute who told a lie on behalf of the Israelites, and despite Rahab's lifestyle she believed God is good, and He would protect His people. Her story was referred to three times in the New Testament, and Rahab's name is in the hall of faith found in Hebrews 11, where people of great faith are listed.

"For we have heard how the Lᴏʀᴅ dried up the water of the Red Sea before you when you came out of Egypt, and what you did to the two kings of the Amorites. . . . And as soon as we heard it, our hearts melted." (Joshua 2:10–11)

Rᴀʜᴀʙ

IDA B. ROBINSON

(1891–1946)

❧

Ida B. Robinson is known as the founder of Mount Sinai Holy Church of America. Her birth name was Ida Bell, and she was born on August 3, 1891, in Hazlehurst, Georgia—the seventh of twelve children born to Robert and Anne Bell. Ida became a Christian when she was a teenager, and her ministry began as a young girl when she led prayer meetings in people's homes.[1]

In 1909 she married Oliver Robinson. They had no children but later adopted Ida's niece. The couple moved to Philadelphia, where they attended a small congregation at Seventeenth and South Streets. Benjamin Smith was the pastor, and Ida began to sing and preach, filling in for Smith in his absence. Ida engaged in street evangelism under the leadership of the United Holy Church of America. In 1919 the church ordained her and assigned her to a small mission church, but Robinson was discouraged that so few opportunities were available for women to serve in

full-time ministry. As an African American woman, she faced continual challenges in fulfilling her call to ministry.

After a time of prayer and fasting, Robinson felt led to launch a new denomination called the Mount Sinai Holy Church of America. In 1924 the state of Pennsylvania granted her a charter for Mount Sinai Holy Church.[2] From its inception, women held roles in leadership, and among the nine officers, six were women. Robinson focused on evangelism and church planting, and the denomination multiplied. By the time of her death, the Mount Sinai Holy Church of America had 84 churches, more than 160 ordained pastors, an accredited school, and mission outreaches in Guyana and Cuba.

"If Mary could carry the
Word of God in her womb,
then I can carry the Word
of God on my lips."

IDA B. ROBINSON[3]

JACKIE ROBINSON

1919–1972

⌣⌣⌣

Jackie Robinson was the first African American Major League Baseball player. Born in 1919 in Cairo, Georgia, Robinson and his four siblings were raised by their single mother, Mallie. The Robinsons were the only African American family in their neighborhood and routinely faced racism in their community.[1]

Growing up, Robinson excelled in sports and at UCLA became the first student to letter in baseball, basketball, football, and track. A lack of finances forced Robinson to leave college and enlist in the military, where after two years he rose to second lieutenant. His military career was cut short after he was court-martialed for his objections to moving to the back of a segregated bus. Eventually he was acquitted of the charges and received an honorable discharge from the military.[2]

In 1945 Robinson played shortstop for a season in the Negro Leagues with the Kansas City Monarchs. Two years later the

president of the Brooklyn Dodgers, Branch Rickey, approached Robinson about joining the team. The major leagues hadn't had an African American player since 1889 when the league segregated. Rickey wanted Robinson both for his athletic talent and for his demeanor. Rickey knew he would be a target for discrimination, but Robinson could confront the challenges with wisdom and dignity.

In 1946 Robinson joined the Montreal Royals—the Dodgers' farm team. Teammates and fans opposed Robinson's presence and acted with a vengeance. Pitchers threw fastballs at his head, base runners spiked him with their cleats, and the crowds shouted vile insults. Robinson and his family received daily threats by mail. During that first year Robinson's wife, Rachel, recalled him getting on his hands and knees every night to pray. Robinson said, "It's the best way to get closer to God."[3]

Despite the constant threats Robinson persisted and led the team with a .349 batting average and forty stolen bases. He was called up from the minors to make his national debut as a first baseman for the Brooklyn Dodgers on April 15, 1947. His success continued, and Robinson won Rookie of the Year and two years later was named Most Valuable Player. During Robinson's ten seasons as a Dodger, they won the pennant six times and won the 1955 World Series. Since 2004, Major League Baseball has acknowledged April 15 as Jackie Robinson Day to commemorate his life and achievement.[4]

"Life is not a spectator sport. If you're going to spend your whole life in the grandstand just watching what goes on, in my opinion you're wasting your life."

JACKIE ROBINSON[5]

J. C. RYLE

1816–1900

〜

J. C. Ryle was born in England on May 10, 1816, to wealthy parents who sent him to Eton and Oxford, where he excelled in sports and academics. Although he was raised in the church, Ryle admitted that early on he had no desire to pray or read his Bible. While in college, he developed a severe respiratory infection, and during his illness he thought about eternity and his relationship with God. Shortly after he recovered he attended church and was moved by a sermon he heard on the theme of grace and a Scripture passage from Ephesians 2:8–9: "For by grace you have been saved through faith. And this is not your own doing; it is the gift of God, not a result of works, so that no one may boast."[1] Ryle later said hearing that passage was the first time he understood what it meant to be saved by grace, and it was then he gave his heart to Christ.

Ryle planned to enter into law or politics. As the oldest son of

a wealthy man, he was poised to inherit a fortune, but then his father's bank crashed, and they were financially ruined. Ryle later said, "I have not the least doubt, it was all for the best. If I had not been ruined, I should never have been a clergyman, never have preached a sermon, or written a tract or book."[2]

On December 21, 1841, Ryle was ordained for ministry. He began his ministry at the Chapel of Ease in Exbury, Hampshire. In 1843 he became rector of St. Thomas's, Winchester, and of Helmingham, Suffolk, the following year. In Helmingham, he was married and widowed twice. In 1861 he married his third wife, Henrietta Amelia Clowes, and they were married until her death in 1889.

In 1880 Ryle became the first bishop of Liverpool. Ryle's writing was a significant part of his ministry, and he published widely. His ministry was marked by his focus on opening churches to meet the expanding urban population. In 1900 he retired at the age of eighty-three, and he died later the same year. Charles Spurgeon described Ryle as "the best man in England."

"Whatever you do for God, do it with all your heart and mind and strength. In other things be moderate, and dread running into extremes. In soul matters fear moderation just as you would fear the plague."

J. C. Ryle[3]

IDA SCUDDER

1870–1960

❦

Ida Scudder was a third-generation medical missionary to India. Born in India on December 9, 1870, as the daughter of American missionaries, she had no plans to pursue medicine or missionary work. Growing up she'd seen the poverty, disease, and famine in India. After college she planned to stay in the United States and get married. Instead, Dwight Moody invited her to attend his Northfield Seminary in Massachusetts, and she pursued her studies there.[1]

In 1890 she returned to India to help her father and ailing mother. During that trip she witnessed three women die in childbirth because their husbands refused her father's medical care and would only allow another woman to tend to their wives. The experience convinced Scudder that God's plan for her was to become a physician and care for the underserved women in India. In 1899 she graduated from Cornell Medical College

as a member of the first class of women allowed as medical students.[2]

A Manhattan banker gifted Scudder with a ten-thousand-dollar grant in memory of his wife. Scudder returned to India with the money and opened a medical dispensary and women's clinic. In the first two years, she treated five thousand patients. In 1902 she opened the Mary Taber Schell Hospital. Scudder had witnessed the overwhelming needs in India and knew she couldn't do it alone, so she focused her attention on opening a medical school for women. Critics told her she'd be lucky to get three applicants, and regulations from the Indian government threatened her work. In 1918, 151 women applied, and there was a waiting list after that. Finally, in 1928 she broke ground on what would become the Vellore Christian Medical Center. Scudder returned to the United States numerous times to raise money for the project.

Scudder died in 1960 at the age of ninety. She never married. Today her legacy continues. In 2003 the Vellore Christian Medical Center was the largest Christian medical facility in the world, with the capacity to care for two thousand inpatients, and its medical school is one of the most prestigious in India.

"Each one of the three wives
had died because there was no
woman doctor to go to them."

Ida Scudder[3]

AMANDA BERRY SMITH

1837–1915

Amanda Berry Smith was a Methodist Holiness preacher, missionary, and founder of an orphanage. She was born into slavery in 1837 to Samuel Berry and Miriam Matthews Berry, and her father eventually gained freedom for the family.[1] Amanda pursued her education by reading the Bible and taking night classes taught by a local school teacher. Later, she worked as a housekeeper near York, Pennsylvania, and married Calvin Devine, who was killed serving in the Union army. She soon remarried, and her second husband, James Smith, a Methodist deacon, died of stomach cancer. Amanda had given birth to five children, but only one survived. Before her thirtieth birthday, she was twice widowed and a single mother, earning money in

domestic work.[2] Reeling from grief and overwhelmed with her circumstances, Amanda drew closer in her relationship to God and was active in the local church.

At Methodist Camp meetings, Amanda became known for her preaching and singing skills. She developed a signature style in her dress, wearing a Quaker bonnet and plain clothing with the intention of focusing on God's will for her life rather than her outward appearance. In 1878 she joined a mission trip to England and later traveled to India and Liberia.[3] About her travels she wrote, "Since then, I have been a widow, and have traveled halfway round the world, and God has ever been faithful. He has never left me a moment; but in all these years I have proved the word true, 'Lo, I am with you always, even to the end.'"[4]

During her time in Africa, she adopted two orphaned girls. In 1890 she returned to the United States, and she became a well-known evangelist for the Woman's Christian Temperance Union in Chicago. In 1899 she fulfilled a lifelong dream and opened the Amanda Smith Orphanage and Industrial Home for Abandoned and Destitute Colored Children in Harvey, Illinois. Smith raised money to keep the orphanage afloat and spent her final years in ministry serving the children at the orphanage. She died in 1915 at the age of seventy-eight.

"I found out that it was not necessary to be a nun or be isolated away off in some deep retirement to have communion with Jesus; but, though your hands are employed in doing your daily business; it is no bar to the soul's communion with Jesus."

AMANDA BERRY SMITH[5]

EDITH STEIN

1891–1942

E dith Stein was a Catholic nun who died in Auschwitz concentration camp in 1942. Stein was born on October 12, 1891, into a Jewish family in Wroclaw, Poland. Her father died when she was a toddler, and her mother was left to run the family lumberyard and raise a large family as a single mother. The youngest of eleven children, Stein flourished in school and graduated first in her class. She focused her studies on phenomenology and received her PhD in philosophy from the University of Freiburg under Edmund Husserl.[1]

Although she had drifted from her Jewish faith, Stein continued to seek answers about God. After reading St. Teresa of Ávila's autobiography, Stein felt she found the truth she'd been seeking. So she converted to Catholicism, which disappointed her mother and several of her Jewish friends. She took a teaching post at the German Institute for Scientific Pedagogy in Münster,

but in April 1933, following the rise of the National Socialists in Germany, she was fired because of her Jewish descent.[2] The following October she entered the Carmelite convent. On April 21, 1935, Stein made her profession of vows and became Teresia Benedicta a Cruce, or Teresa Benedicta of the Cross.

As anti-Semitism grew in Germany, she realized she was a liability to her faith community. In 1938 she was transferred to the Carmelite convent at Echt, Holland, for safety reasons. It was there that she wrote *The Science of the Cross* and *Ways to Know God*, which would become her most important writings. On August 2, 1942, Edith and her sister Rosa were arrested by the Gestapo and transferred to Auschwitz concentration camp. The sisters arrived on August 7 and died in Auschwitz's gas chamber on August 9. Her writings fill seventeen volumes, including translations of Cardinal Newman's diaries and Thomas Aquinas's *Quaestiones disputatae de veritate*.[3] Today, Stein is acknowledged as a martyr and saint of the Roman Catholic Church. In 1998 she was canonized by Pope John Paul II and is known as St. Teresa Benedict of the Cross.[4]

"I keep thinking of Queen Esther who was taken away from her people precisely because God wanted her to plead with the king on behalf of her nation. I am a very poor and powerless little Esther, but the King who has chosen me is infinitely great and merciful. This is a great comfort."

EDITH STEIN[5]

CLARA SWAIN

1834–1910

~⚬~

Clara Swain is known as the "pioneer woman physician in India." She was born in 1834, the youngest of ten children, in Elmira, New York. Like many women in the late nineteenth century, Swain started her work life as a schoolteacher, but she changed careers when she began training at the Castile Sanitarium. After completing a three-year program, she enrolled at Woman's Medical College in Philadelphia and graduated in the spring of 1869.[1] She and Isabella Thoburn were the first women to be sponsored for overseas missionary work by the newly founded Women's Foreign Missionary Society of the Methodist Episcopal Church. They set sail from New York on November 3, 1869, and arrived in India on January 20, 1870.

Upon arrival she served high-caste women whose religion forbade them from being treated by male physicians. Swain believed it was God's will for her to serve there, and she was committed to

a career of service rather than personal distinction or notoriety. In an early letter home, she wrote, "India is far more beautiful than I expected and far more ugly."[2] The orphanages and clinics were in constant need of Swain's medical services. She immediately recognized the need for more medical personnel, so she enlisted sixteen girls from the orphanage and taught them the basics of medical care. Swain spent the next twenty-seven years treating women and children there and simultaneously sharing her Christian faith.

Eventually, the Clara Swain Hospital would open in Bareilly, India. At the height of the hospital's success, 350 patient beds were in use, and it was the leading institution for nursing education in northern India.[3] In April 1908 Swain returned to the United States and stayed at the sanitarium in Castile, New York. Her health was declining, and she died on December 25, 1910. A friend collected and compiled the letters Swain had written over the years and published them as *A Glimpse of India.* Swain served the people of India and paved the way for women as medical missionaries.

"Where is this place of greatest need which God wants me to fill?"

Clara Swain[4]

JONI EARECKSON TADA

1949–present

In 1967 Joni Eareckson Tada dove into the Chesapeake Bay and sustained injuries that left her a quadriplegic. In the months and years of recovery that followed, Joni experienced deep depression and doubt, but her faith in God motivated her to use her disability for God's glory. During occupational therapy, Joni learned to paint with a brush in her mouth and began selling her artwork. In 1974 she told her story on *Today* and started gaining a national audience. Two years later she published her autobiography, *Joni: An Unforgettable Story,* which sold more than five million copies and was translated into thirty-eight languages.[1]

To help as many people as possible, Joni opened Joni and Friends—a Christian ministry dedicated to serving people

with disabilities by sharing the gospel and providing practical resources. Joni and Friends's mission statement is "To glorify God as we communicate the Gospel and mobilize the global church to evangelize, disciple, and serve people living with disability."[2] In 1994 she founded Wheels for the World, which provides wheelchairs for people in need. In 2014 the organization celebrated the milestone of gifting one hundred thousand wheelchairs to people in Ghana.

Throughout her life, Joni has spoken honestly about suffering in the context of her faith. In addition to the medical challenges that come with her paralysis, Joni underwent treatment for cancer in 2010 and 2018. She's also lived with chronic pain so severe she's described it as "jaw splitting."[3] But despite Joni's medical challenges and decades of suffering, she's consistently encouraged others to seek Jesus amid suffering. She wrote, "Always and always I want to be in submission to the Father and obedient to the Word of Jesus—knowing full well that if I had everything else in life and lacked that, I would have nothing at all."[4]

In 1982 she married Ken Tada, and they live in Calabasas, California. For more than forty years, Tada has been a speaker, writer, and advocate for people with disabilities. She's written more than forty books and received numerous honors and awards.

"Only God is capable of telling us what our rights and needs are. You have to surrender that right to Him."

Joni Eareckson Tada[5]

JAMES HUDSON TAYLOR

1832–1905

❧

James Hudson Taylor was born in Barnsley, Yorkshire, England, on May 21, 1832. His parents were godly people who wanted their son to serve Christ. At seventeen, Hudson Taylor felt called to full-time Christian ministry, and he spent the next three years preparing to serve. He studied rudimentary medicine and the Mandarin language, and he immersed himself in Bible study and prayer.[1] On September 19, 1853, he set sail for China with the Chinese Evangelical Society.

Hudson Taylor's goal was to serve the people, so he set out with colleague Joseph Edkins, and they sailed down the Huangpu River handing out Bibles and religious tracts. In 1857 the Chinese Evangelical Society was no longer able to pay its missionaries,

so Hudson Taylor branched out on his own and trusted God to provide for his needs. Shortly after, he married Maria Dyer—a daughter of missionaries.

In Ninpo, Hudson Taylor pastored a small church that grew to twenty-one members. In 1861 he became sick and returned to England for treatment. While he recovered he worked on translating the Bible into Chinese, trained to be a midwife, and recruited more missionaries to China. His goal was to recruit twenty-four.[2]

Hudson Taylor was worried that he'd send missionaries into harm's way, but he was equally concerned that the Chinese should have the opportunity to hear the gospel. He experienced months of internal conflict and wrote that he felt he might "lose his mind." A friend invited him to the South Coast of England for a retreat, and it was there his anxiety lifted. He wrote, "There, the Lord conquered my unbelief, and I surrendered myself to God for this service. I told him that all responsibility as to the issues and consequences must rest with him; that as his servant, it was mine to obey and to follow him."[3]

Hudson Taylor's organization would be called the China Inland Mission. Missionaries wouldn't have a guaranteed salary, and they wouldn't solicit funds—they would rely on God to meet their needs. Today, the organization operates with the same philosophy and is known as the Overseas Missionary Fellowship.[4]

"All God's giants have been
weak men, who did great things
for God because they reckoned
on His being with them."

JAMES HUDSON TAYLOR[5]

ALEXANDER WALTERS

1858–1917

A lexander Walters rose from slavery to become a bishop in the African Methodist Episcopal Zion Church and a leading voice in civil rights. In 1858 Walters was born into slavery—the sixth of eight children—in Bardstown, Kentucky. When Walters was seven, he was freed from slavery through the Thirteenth Amendment. By his tenth birthday, Walters had so excelled in his studies that he was awarded a full scholarship by the African Episcopal Zion Church to enroll in private schooling. When he was nineteen years old, Walters received his license to preach and began his ministry in Indianapolis, Indiana. In 1892 he was serving as a minister at the Seventh District of the African Methodist Episcopal Zion Church when he was named bishop.[1]

In 1898 Bishop Walters pivoted his attention to civil rights issues. While serving at Mother Zion Church in Harlem, New York, Walters met T. Thomas Fortune, editor of the *New York Age*. Together, they founded the National Afro-American Council, and Walters served as president. The goal was to address Jim Crow laws, lynching, and racial discrimination. The organization lasted only three years but served as a launchpad for future endeavors. Later, they founded the Afro-American Council (AAC). The organization focused on challenging racially discriminatory legislation focusing on the "separate but equal" ruling in the 1896 *Plessy vs. Ferguson* case.[2]

By 1897 Walters was working with W. E. B. Du Bois in the Niagara Movement, which later became the National Association for the Advancement of Colored People (NAACP). Walters became its vice president in 1911. Until his death in 1917, Walters remained an active leader in the African Methodist Episcopal Zion Church and a leading voice in the fight for civil rights.

"In the dark days of slavery when a platform was needed for the Negro to plead his own cause, notwithstanding the threatening of slave-holders and their sympathizers in the North and South, Zion Church gave to the anti-slavery advocates a platform."

Alexander Walters[3]

ISAAC WATTS

1674–1748

Isaac Watts is known as the "Father of English Hymnody." He wrote more than 750 hymns, including the well-known classics "Joy to the World" and "When I Survey the Wondrous Cross." Watts was born in 1674, and at the time of his birth, his father was in prison for refusing to embrace the established Church of England. His father's courage stuck with Watts.[1]

Watts showed an aptitude for learning at a young age. By age four he was learning Latin and later studied Greek, French, and Hebrew. He could've attended Oxford or Cambridge, but doing so would've put him on the path to Anglican ministry. Instead, Watts traveled to London and studied at a nonconformist academy. In 1702 he became pastor at a Congregational Chapel in London, but the following year he began experiencing mental health issues—a condition he would struggle with for the rest of his life and would force him to resign his pastoral post in 1712.

In 1707 Watts released *Hymns and Spiritual Songs*, which contained "When I Survey the Wondrous Cross," one of the most well-known English hymns in history. Although Lutherans had been singing hymns for a hundred years, John Calvin had encouraged the singing of metrical psalms, where each psalm is rendered into a specific rhythmic form known as "common meter," and English Protestants obliged. Watts wasn't opposed to metrical psalms, but he wanted more passion in them. He said, "They ought to be translated in such a manner as we have reason to believe David would have composed them if he had lived in our day."[2]

In 1719 Watts published *Psalms of David Imitated in the Language of the New Testament*. Critics complained they couldn't recognize the psalms in Watts's new work, but Watts stood his ground and was unapologetic about the looser paraphrase. In places where the psalmist spoke of his enemies, Watts instead referred to spiritual enemies such as sin, temptation, and Satan. In regards to the criticism he received, he said, "Where the flights of his faith and love are sublime, I have often sunk the expressions within the reach of an ordinary Christian."[3]

Although Watts is best known for his hymns, his legacy includes a large body of writing, including thirty theological treatises; three volumes of sermons; essays on philosophy, astronomy, and psychology; the first children's hymnal; and a textbook on logic. He died in 1748 in Stoke Newington, Great Britain.

Joy to the world, the Lord is come

Let earth receive her King

Let every heart,

prepare him room

And heaven and nature sing.

ISAAC WATTS

SUSANNA WESLEY

1669–1742

~~~❦~~~

Susanna Wesley, the mother of John and Charles, is known as the "Mother of Methodism." Born on January 20, 1669, she was the youngest of twenty-five children. When she was nineteen years old, she married Samuel Wesley, a pastor for the Church of England, and they had nineteen children—ten of whom survived.

Between her role as a preacher's wife and mother to a large family, Wesley managed a busy household and was known for her exemplary organizational skills. She took on the role of educating her children and taught them the classics, reading, writing, and arithmetic. They also memorized Scripture and learned good manners.[1] With such a large family, Wesley intentionally set apart time to be alone with each child so they would have her undivided attention.[2]

When her husband traveled, Wesley led worship services

in her home—a role that her husband disapproved of. It wasn't common for a woman to lead prayer or worship in the early eighteenth century, and Wesley acknowledged the tension. She said, "As to its looking particular [unseemly], I grant that it does, but so does almost everything that is serious, or that may anyway advance the glory of God or the salvation of souls, if it be performed out of a pulpit, or in the way of common conversation."[3]

Wesley's role in her home and unwavering commitment to her children set the tone for sons Charles and John and the other Wesley children. John would become the founder of Methodism, and Charles composed more than 6,500 hymns and is one of the most well-known English poets of his time. The Reverend Alfred Day said, "Susanna Wesley is a major difference-maker. And the differences that she made have lived on from the history of 17th and 18th century well into the present moment because of the sons that she raised."[4] Susanna Wesley never preached from the pulpit, founded a denomination, or wrote a book, but her legacy continues through the children she raised.

"I am content to fill a little

space if God be glorified."

Susanna Wesley[5]

PHILLIS WHEATLEY

1753–1784

On July 11, 1761, Phillis Wheatley arrived in America aboard the *Phillis*. When she disembarked, the child was naked, malnourished, and ill. Because she was missing two front teeth, they estimated she was seven years old. Of the ninety-six Africans who boarded the vessel, only seventy-five survived the crossing—and those who survived were sold into slavery once they arrived in Boston. John Wheatley, a prominent Boston tailor and merchant, and his wife, Susanna, bought the child and named her Phillis after the ship she arrived on.[1]

As a young girl, Phillis was treated well by the Wheatley family. She was spared the tasks of most eighteenth-century slaves and was educated along with the Wheatley children. She was also taught the tenets of Christianity, and in 1771 Phillis was baptized. Her newfound faith led her to believe that God's

providence had led her to America, where she would come to know Jesus—a sentiment that was widely criticized.

Although Phillis was outspoken against slavery, she continued to be maligned for giving thanks to God for her saving grace. Despite the criticism, Phillis continued to write and was published in numerous newspapers. Even though she'd become well-known, she struggled to find a publisher. In 1773 she traveled to London, where she published her first collection of poems, *Poems on Various Subjects, Religious and Moral*. It was the first book published by a black woman in America.[2]

Although the Wheatleys had treated her well as a child, Phillis was left out of the family's estate and will. Still in search of a publisher who would publish her second volume of work, she married John Peters, a grocer in Boston who was eventually put in prison for his debt. The couple's two children died as infants. Wheatley died when she was thirty-one, and although not confirmed, some believe it was during childbirth. Despite being penniless and alone, after years of suffering, Wheatley was outspoken about her belief in God's goodness and mercy.

"The world is a severe schoolmaster, for its frowns are less dangerous than its smiles and flatteries, and it is a difficult task to keep in the path of wisdom."

PHILLIS WHEATLEY[3]

JOHN WYCLIFFE

c. 1330–1384

❧

John Wycliffe was a leading theologian in his era, but his critics were so threatened by his teaching that they labeled him a heretic. Forty-three years after his death, his body was exhumed and burned and his ashes thrown into the River Swift.[1]

Wycliffe was born on a sheep farm two hundred miles from London around 1330. He was educated at Oxford University and obtained his doctorate in 1372, earning a reputation as a prominent philosopher and theologian. His opinions about the papacy beckoned both supporters and critics. Wycliffe was outspoken about his belief that the Holy Scriptures were the only trustworthy guide about the teachings of God and that Christians should rely on their Bibles rather than the teaching of popes and clerics.

Wycliffe condemned the doctrine of transubstantiation, challenged the Catholic Church's use of indulgences, and spoke out against the private confession of sins to a priest—maintaining no

third party was necessary but that confession was to be between a believer and his God. Wycliffe believed that all people should have a copy of the Scriptures in their native language and began translating the Bible into English along with his friend John Purvey. Church leadership was adamantly opposed to Wycliffe's translation efforts, but he was unmoved, saying, "Englishmen learn Christ's law best in English. Moses heard God's law in his own tongue; so did Christ's apostles."[2]

Wycliffe wrote and published his views in numerous tracts. He believed that England should be ruled by the monarchy, with no interference from the church. He said, "England belongs to no pope. The pope is but a man, subject to sin, but Christ is the Lord of Lords and this kingdom is to be held directly and solely of Christ alone."[3]

Wycliffe was attending a Christmas Mass in 1384 when he suffered a stroke. He died a week later on December 31, 1384. Although he passed before the Bible translation was finished, his friend Purvey finished what we know today as the "Wycliffe Bible."[4] After his death, Wycliffe was called the "Morning Star of the Protestant Reformation."[5]

"Trust wholly in Christ; rely altogether on his sufferings; beware of seeking to be justified in any other way than by his righteousness."

JOHN WYCLIFFE[6]

LOUIS ZAMPERINI

1917–2014

Louis Zamperini was a World War II veteran and Olympic distance runner. Zamperini was born to Italian immigrants on January 26, 1917, in Olean, New York,[1] but grew up in Torrance, California. His older brother, Pete, encouraged him to try out for the track team, and Zamperini learned he excelled as a runner. He set the record for running a mile in 4 minutes and 21.2 seconds, and his track achievements earned him a scholarship to the University of Southern California. In 1936 he qualified for the Olympics in Berlin while still a teenager. Zamperini fell short of a gold medal, but he returned from the Olympics a revered athlete and continued setting college records.

In September 1941 Zamperini enlisted in the army and quickly rose to second lieutenant, serving as an Army Air Corpsman in World War II. In May 1943 his plane crashed into the Pacific Ocean. For the next forty-seven days, Zamperini and two other

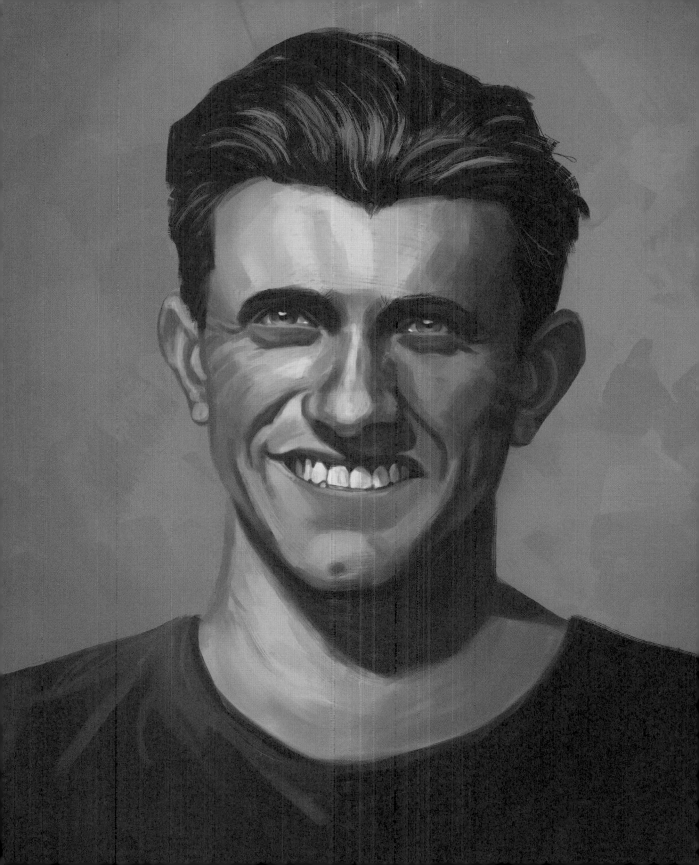

survivors floated on a raft. The Japanese located the men, and Zamperini was captured and taken as a prisoner of war. For more than two years, Zamperini was held captive and tortured. As an American Olympian, he was a target of abuse. Japanese corporal Mutsuhiro Watanabe, who was known as the "Bird," was especially cruel to Zamperini.[2]

In 1945 the war ended, and Zamperini was set free, but his troubles weren't over. Once home he suffered from post-traumatic stress, nightmares, and alcoholism that almost ended his marriage. Zamperini credits his turnaround to becoming a Christian after hearing the gospel at a Billy Graham Crusade. About his newfound faith Zamperini said, "I felt this perfect calm, a peace. The Bible calls it the peace that passeth all understanding. I knew then that I was through getting drunk, smoking, and chasing around. I also knew I'd forgiven all my prison guards, including the Bird. Boy, that's something. So I got up, went home, and that was the first night in four years that I didn't have a nightmare. And I haven't had one since."[3]

Zamperini spent the latter years of his life sharing his story and Christian faith, placing a special focus on the message of forgiveness. He died on July 2, 2014, at the age of ninety-seven.

"All I want to tell young people is that you're not going to be anything in life unless you learn to commit to a goal. You have to reach deep within yourself to see if you are willing to make the sacrifices."

LOUIS ZAMPERINI[4]

NOTES

SUSAN B. ANTHONY

1. Nancy Hayward, "Susan B. Anthony," National Women's History Museum, https://www.womenshistory.org/education-resources/biographies/susan-b-anthony.
2. "Susan B. Anthony," History.com. March 9, 2010, https://www.history.com/topics/womens-history/susan-b-anthony.

ANNE ASKEW

1. Michelle DeRusha, *50 Women Every Christian Should Know: Learning from Heroines of the Faith* (Grand Rapids: Baker Books, 2014), 66–67.
2. Derek Wilson, "Tortured for Her Faith: Anne Askew, the Protestant Martyr Who Loved Scripture," Christianity Today, April 18, 2018, https://www.christiantoday.com/article/tortured-for-her-faith-anne-askew-the-protestant-martyr-who-loved-scripture/128517.htm.
3. DeRusha, *50 Women*, 67.
4. David Crowther, "Anne Askew, Martyr and Author," The History of England, https://thehistoryofengland.co.uk/resource/anne-askew-martyr-and-author/.

ELIZABETH BLACKWELL

1. Janice P. Nimura, *The Doctors Blackwell: How Two Pioneering Sisters Brought Medicine to Women—and Women to Medicine* (New York: W. W. Norton and Co., 2021), 26.
2. Nimura, *Doctors Blackwell*, 3.
3. Nimura, *Doctors Blackwell*, 268.
4. Jamie Ducharme, "Who Is Elizabeth Blackwell? Why Google Is Celebrating the Pioneer," Time, February 3, 2018, https://time.com/5131961/elizabeth-blackwell-facts/.

WILLIAM BOOTH

1. "William Booth," Christianity Today, https://www.christianitytoday.com/history/people/activists/william-booth.html.
2. "The Best 18 Quotes from William Booth," Caring Magazine, July 2, 2020, https://caringmagazine.org/the-best-18-quotes-from-william-booth/.
3. "History of the Salvation Army," The Salvation Army, https://www.salvationarmyusa.org/usn/history-of-the-salvation-army/.
4. "Best 18 Quotes."

DAVID BRAINERD

1. "David Brainerd," Banner of Truth, https://banneroftruth.org/us/about/banner-authors/david-brainerd/.

2. "Brainerd, David (1718–1747)," Boston University School of Theology, https://www.bu.edu/missiology/missionary-biography/a-c/brainerd-david-1718-1747/.
3. "Brainerd, David (1718–1747)."
4. David Brainerd, *The Life and Diary of David Brainerd* (Readaclassic.com, USA, 2010), 40.

LUCY GOODE BROOKS

1. "Lucy Goode Brooks (1818–1900)," Virginia Changemakers, https://edu.lva.virginia.gov/changemakers/items/show/10.
2. Olympia Meola, "Lucy Goode Brooks," Richmond Times-Dispatch, September 19, 2019, https://richmond.com/lucy-goode-brooks/article_3917d1d6-d712-56f0-ae80-830d9191588c.html.
3. "Brooks, Lucy Goode (1818–1900)," Encyclopedia Virginia, https://encyclopediavirginia.org/entries/brooks-lucy-goode-1818-1900/.
4. Susan Winiecki, "The First Gabriel Week," Richmond Magazine, August 21, 2018, https://richmondmagazine.com/news/richmond-history/gabriel-week-2018/.

JOHN BUNYAN

1. "John Bunyan," Banner of Truth, https://banneroftruth.org/us/about/banner-authors/john-bunyan/.
2. "John Bunyan," Banner of Truth, https://banneroftruth.org/us/about/banner-authors/john-bunyan/.
3. "John Bunyan," Christianity Today, https://www.christianitytoday.com/history/people/musiciansartistsandwriters/john-bunyan.html.

JOSEPHINE BUTLER

1. Josephine E. Butler, Josephine Butler: An Autobiographical Memoir, ed. George Johnson and Lucy Johnson (London: J. W. Aerosmith, 1909), 6.
2. Kimi Harris, "Jesus Befriended Prostitutes. So This Victorian-Era Woman Did Too," Christianity Today, https://www.christianitytoday.com/history/2018/july/josephine-butler-victorian-advocate-for-prostitutes-history.html.
3. Harris, "Jesus Befriended Prostitutes."
4. Harris.
5. Harris.
6. Butler, *Josephine Butler: An Autobiographical Memoir*, 155.

WILLIAM CAREY

1. Vishal Mangalwadi and Ruth Mangalwadi, *The Legacy of William Carey: A Model for the Transformation of a Culture* (Wheaton: Crossway, 1999), 133–34.

2. "William Carey," Christianity Today, https://www
.christianitytoday.com/history/people/missionaries
/william-carey.html.

3. "William Carey."

4. "William Carey."

CHARLES COLSON

1. Eric Metaxas, *Seven Men and the Secret of Their Greatness*
(Nashville: Thomas Nelson, 2013), 166.

2. Tim Weiner, "Charles W. Colson, Watergate Felon Who Became
Evangelical Leader, Dies at 80," New York Times, April 21, 2012,
https://www.nytimes.com/2012/04/22/us/politics/charles-w
-colson-watergate-felon-who-became-evangelical-leader-dies
-at-80.html.

3. "Our Founder, Chuck Colson," Prison Fellowship, https://www.
prisonfellowship.org/archivedpages/chuckcolson
/?mwm_id=295733995344&sc=PGNWAAG190104012.

DOROTHY DAY

1. "Dorothy Day," Biography.com, July 6, 2020, https://www.
biography.com/writer/dorothy-day.

2. Casey Cep, "Dorothy Day's Radical Faith," New Yorker,
April 6, 2020, https://www.newyorker.com/magazine/2020
/04/13/dorothy-days-radical-faith?source=search_google
_dsa_paid&gclid=EAIaIQobChMIgJfvjf2X8QIVAqCGCh3Yx
QodEAAYASAAEgJS7PD_BwE.

3. Brian Orme, "21 Dorothy Day Quotes That Will Inspire You to
Love Deeper," Church Leaders, September 25, 2015, https://
churchleaders.com/daily-buzz/263107-21-dorothy-day-quotes
-will-inspire-love-deeper.html.

JIM ELLIOT

1. Sam Roberts, "Elisabeth Elliot, Tenacious Missionary in Face of
Tragedy, Dies at 88," New York Times, June 18, 2015, https://
www.nytimes.com/2015/06/18/us/elisabeth-elliot-tenacious
-missionary-to-ecuador-dies-at-88.html.

2. Justin Taylor, "They Were No Fools: The Martyrdom of Jim Elliot
and Four Other Missionaries," Gospel Coalition, January 8, 2016,
https://www.thegospelcoalition.org/blogs/justin-taylor/they
-were-no-fools-60-years-ago-today-the-martyrdom-of-jim
-elliot-and-four-other-missionaries/.

3. Dargan Thompson, "Jim Elliot Quotes That Will Change the Way
You Think About Sacrifice," Relevant, January 8, 2016, https://
www.relevantmagazine.com/faith/jim-elliot-quotes-will-change
-way-you-think-about-sacrifice/.

ESTHER

1. The Charles F. Stanley Life Principles Bible, NKJV (Nashville:
Thomas Nelson, 2005), 573.

CHARLES FINNEY

1. "Charles Finney," PBS, https://www.pbs.org/wgbh/pages
/frontline/godinamerica/people/charles-finney.html.

2. "Charles Finney," Christianity Today, https://www.
christianitytoday.com/history/people/evangelistsandapologists
/charles-finney.html.

3. Charles Finney, *Lectures on Revivals of Religion* (2014).

ELIZABETH FRY

1. "Elizabeth Fry," Christianity Today, https://www.christianitytoday
.com/history/people/activists/elizabeth-fry.html.

2. DeRusha, *50 Women*, 112.

3. "Elizabeth Fry."

4. Elizabeth Gurney Fry and Katharine Fry, *Memoir of the Life of
Elizabeth Fry: With Extracts from Her Journals and Letters*
(Charleston, SC: Nabu Press, 2010).

HENRY HIGHLAND GARNET

1. Paul Ortiz, "One of History's Foremost Anti-Slavery Organizers
Is Often Left Out of the Black History Month Story," Time,
January 31, 2018, https://time.com/5124917/black-history-month
-henry-highland-garnet/.

2. Paul Ortiz, "One of History's Foremost Anti-Slavery Organizers
Is Often Left Out of the Black History Month Story," Time,
January 31, 2018, https://time.com/5124917/black-history-month
-henry-highland-garnet/.

GEORGE FRIDERIC HANDEL

1. "George Frideric Handel: A Brief Biography of the Man and the
Early Days of Messiah," The Tabernacle Choir at Temple Square,
https://www.thetabernaclechoir.org/messiah/george-frideric
-handel-a-brief-history.html.

2. "George Frideric Handel: A Brief Biography of the Man and the
Early Days of Messiah," The Tabernacle Choir at Temple Square,
https://www.thetabernaclechoir.org/messiah/george-frideric
-handel-a-brief-history.html.

3. "George Frideric Handel: A Brief Biography of the Man and the
Early Days of Messiah," The Tabernacle Choir at Temple Square,
https://www.thetabernaclechoir.org/messiah/george-frideric
-handel-a-brief-history.html.

MAHALIA JACKSON

1. Francis Ward, "From the Archives: Mahalia Jackson, Renowned
Gospel Singer, Dies at 60," Los Angeles Times, January 28, 1972,
https://www.latimes.com/local/obituaries/archives/la-me
-mahalia-jackson-19720128-story.html.

2. Ward, "From the Archives."

3. Sonari Glinton, "Mahalia Jackson: Voice of the Civil Rights
Movement," NPR, February 8, 2010, https://www.npr.org
/templates/story/story.php?storyId=123498527.

4. "Mahalia Jackson, Gospel Singer and a Civil Rights Symbol, Dies,"
New York Times, January 28, 1972, https://www.nytimes.com
/1972/01/28/archives/mahalia-jackson-gospel-singer-and-a
-civil-rights-symbol-dies.html?.?mc=aud_dev&ad-keywords
=auddevgate&gclid=EAIaIQobChMI1dLO87_C8QIVk8iUCR2wswz
CEAMYASAAEgLe9fD_BwE&gclsrc=aw.ds.

JOAN OF ARC

1. Mark Galli and Ted Olsen, *131 Christians Everyone Should Know*
(Nashville: B&H Publishing, 2000), 215.

2. Galli and Olsen, *131 Christians Everyone Should Know*, 214.

ABSALOM JONES

1. Matt Gardner, "I Look in the Mirror, I See Absalom Jones,"
Anglican Journal, February 1, 2021, https://www.

anglicanjournal.com/i-look-in-the-mirror-i-see-absalom
-jones/.

2. "Absalom Jones," Christian History Institute, https://
christianhistoryinstitute.org/magazine/article/absalom-jones.

3. "Absalom Jones."

4. "Absalom Jones."

ADONIRAM JUDSON

1. Nathan Finn, "Missionaries You Should Know: Adoniram
Judson," IMB, March 27, 2018, https://www.imb.org/2018/03/27
/missionaries-you-should-know-adoniram-judson/.

2. Finn, "Missionaries You Should Know."

3. "Adoniram Judson (1788–1850)," Missions Box, February 20, 2018,
https://missionsbox.org/missionary-bio/adoniram-judson
-1788-1850/.

4. "Adoniram Judson (1788–1850)."

5. "Adoniram Judson (1788–1850)."

ANN HASSELTINE JUDSON

1. "Adoniram Judson (1788–1850)."

2. Michael A. G. Haykin, "Remembering Ann Judson 190 Years
Later," Crossway, October 24, 2016, https://www.crossway.org
/articles/remembering-ann-judson-190-years-later/.

3. Haykin, "Remembering Ann Judson."

4. Sharon James, "The Life and Significance of Ann Hasseltine
Judson (1789–1826)," Southern Equip, https://equip.sbts.edu
/publications/journals/journal-of-missions/sbjme-12-fall/the
-life-and-significance-of-ann-hasseltine-judson-1789-1826/.

CORETTA SCOTT KING

1. "About Mrs. King," The King Center, https://thekingcenter.org
/about-tkc/about-mrs-king/.

2. "Happy Birthday! Coretta Scott King Quotes That Will Brighten
Your Day," NewsOne, April 27, 2021, https://newsone.com
/playlist/coretta-scott-king-birthday-quotes/item/3.

PHOEBE KNAPP

1. Diane Severance and Dan Graves, "Phoebe Palmer Knapp: Rich,
Beautiful, Charitable," Christianity.com, May 3, 2010, https://
www.christianity.com/church/church-history/timeline
/1801-1900/phoebe-palmer-knapp-rich-beautiful-charitable
-11630455.html.

2. Stephen Flick, "Phoebe Palmer Knapp (1839–1908),"
Christian Heritage Fellowship, July 8, 2021, https://
christianheritagefellowship.com/phoebe-palmer-knapp
-1839-1908/.

JOHN LEWIS

1. "John Lewis," Biography.com, January 19, 2018, https://www.
biography.com/political-figure/john-lewis.

2. Jay Reeves, "Religious Faith Was a Lifelong Constant for Rep.
John Lewis," ABC News, July 18, 2020, https://abcnews.go.com
/US/wireStory/religious-faith-lifelong-constant-rep-john
-lewis-71858329.

3. Katharine Q. Seelye, "John Lewis, Towering Figure of Civil
Rights Era, Dies at 80," New York Times, July 17, 2020, https://
www.nytimes.com/2020/07/17/us/john-lewis-dead.html.

4. Joshua Bote, "'Get in Good Trouble, Necessary Trouble': Rep. John
Lewis in His Own Words," USA Today, July 18, 2020, https://www.
usatoday.com/story/news/politics/2020/07/18/rep-john-lewis
-most-memorable-quotes-get-good-trouble/5464148002/.

MARY LYON

1. "Mary Lyon," Mount Holyoke College, https://www.mtholyoke
.edu/175/gallery/mary-lyon.

2. "Daily Life at Mount Holyoke," Mount Holyoke College, https://
www.mtholyoke.edu/marylyon/dailylife.

3. "More Quotes by Mary Lyon," Forbes, https://www.forbes.com
/quotes/author/mary-lyon/.

NELSON MANDELA

1. Bill Keller, "Nelson Mandela, South Africa's Liberator as Prisoner
and President, Dies at 95," New York Times, December 5, 2013,
https://www.nytimes.com/2013/12/06/world/africa/nelson
-mandela_obit.html.

2. Keller.

JUSTIN MARTYR

1. Galli and Olsen, 131 Christians Everyone Should Know, 49.

2. Galli and Olsen, 131 Christians Everyone Should Know, 50.

3. Galli and Olsen, 131 Christians Everyone Should Know, 51.

MARY, MOTHER OF JESUS

1. The Charles F. Stanley Life Principles Bible, NKJV (Nashville:
Thomas Nelson, 2005).

WANG MING-DAO

1. John Gill, "Wang Ming-Dao (1900–1991): Faithful amid Political
Coercion, Gospel Coalition, August 3, 2018, https://www.
thegospelcoalition.org/article/wang-ming-dao-faithful
-political-coercion/.

2. Gill, "Wang Ming-Dao (1900–1991)."

3. Gill, "Wang Ming-Dao (1900–1991)."

4. G. Wright Doyle and Yading Li, "Wang Mingdao," Biographical
Dictionary of Chinese Christianity, http://bdcconline.net/en
/stories/wang-mingdao.

HANNAH MORE

1. DeRusha, 50 Women, 98–101.

2. DeRusha, 50 Women, 103.

LUCRETIA MOTT

1. "Lucretia Mott," History.com, December 2, 2009, https://www.
history.com/topics/womens-history/lucretia-mott.

2. "Lucretia Mott."

3. "Lucretia Mott."

4. Nicole Sazegar, "Lucretia Mott's Quotes Remind Us to Keep
Fighting for Our Rights," Entity, September 29, 2017, https://
www.entitymag.com/lucretia-mott-quotes-rights/.

WATCHMAN NEE

1. "Watchman Nee's Life and Ministry," Living Stream Ministry,
https://www.watchmannee.org/life-ministry.html.

2. "Everything for the Lord: Watchman Nee (1901–1972)," Christian History Institute, https://christianhistoryinstitute .org/magazine/article/everything-for-the-lord-watchman-nee.

3. See https://www.watchmannee.org/.

4. Watchman Nee, *The Normal Christian Life* (Carol Stream, IL: Tyndale House, 1957), 4.

FLANNERY O'CONNOR

1. Brad Gooch, *Flannery: A Life of Flannery O'Connor* (New York: Hachette, 2009), 18.

2. Gooch, *Flannery.*

3. Flannery O'Connor, *A Prayer Journal* (New York: Farrar, Straus & Giroux, 2013), 10.

4. O'Connor, *Prayer Journal.*

5. O'Connor, *Prayer Journal*, 36.

IDA B. ROBINSON

1. Priscilla Pope-Levison, "Ida Bell Robinson (1891–1946)," Black Past, January 19, 2007, https://www.blackpast.org/african -american-history/robinson-ida-bell-1891-1946/.

2. "Founder, Senior Bishop & First President," http:// mtsinaiholychurch.org/images/Ida.pdf.

3. Wayne Warner, "Bishop Ida Robinson," Charisma, https://www. charismamag.com/site-archives/24-uncategorised/9481 -bishop-ida-robinson.

JACKIE ROBINSON

1. "Jackie Robinson," National Baseball Hall of Fame, https:// baseballhall.org/hall-of-famers/robinson-jackie.

2. "Jackie Robinson," National Baseball Hall of Fame, https:// baseballhall.org/hall-of-famers/robinson-jackie.

3. Chris Lamb and Ed Henry, "Jackie Robinson's 100th Birthday: His Faith in God Was the Secret Ingredient to His Success," Fox News, January 28, 2019, https://www.foxnews.com/opinion /jackie-robinsons-100th-birthday-his-faith-in-god-was-the -secret-ingredient-to-his-success.

4. "Jackie Robinson Day," MLB Community, https://www.mlb.com /mlb-community/jackie-robinson-day.

5. "Quotes," Jackie Robinson, https://www.jackierobinson.com /quotes/.

J. C. RYLE

1. David Holloway, "J C Ryle: The Man, the Minister and the Missionary," https://www.christian.org.uk/wp-content /uploads/j-c-ryle.pdf.

2. "J. C. Ryle," Banner of Truth, https://banneroftruth.org/us /about/banner-authors/j-c-ryle/.

3. J. C. Ryle, *Practical Religion.*

IDA SCUDDER

1. "Ida Scudder," The Scudder Association Foundation, https:// scudder.org/about/history/india-medical-missions/ida -scudder-story/.

2. "Ida Scudder."

3. Dorothy Clarke Wilson, "The Legacy of Ida S. Scudder," International Bulletin of Missionary Research, January 1987, http://www. internationalbulletin.org/issues/1987-01/1987-01-026-wilson.pdf.

AMANDA BERRY SMITH

1. "Amanda Berry Smith," Southern Methodist University, https:// www.smu.edu/Bridwell/SpecialCollectionsandArchives /Exhibitions/FiftyWomen/19thCenturyAmericans /AmandaSmith.

2. Jamie Janosz, *When Others Shuddered: Eight Women Who Refused to Give Up* (Chicago: Moody Publishers, 2014).

3. "Smith, Amanda [Berry] (1837–1915)," Boston University School of Theology, http://www.bu.edu/missiology/missionary -biography/r-s/smith-amanda-berry-1837-1915/.

4. Janosz, *When Others Shuddered.*

5. Janosz, *When Others Shuddered.*

EDITH STEIN

1. "Edith Stein," Loyola University Chicago, https://www.luc.edu /catholicstudies/newsevents/featuredintellectual/archive /name.243268.en.shtml.

2. "Edith Stein," Stanford Encyclopedia of Philosophy, March 18, 2020, https://plato.stanford.edu/entries/stein/.

3. "Edith Stein," Loyola University Chicago.

4. "The Saintly Life of Edith Stein and Solidarity," United States Conference of Catholic Bishops, https://www.usccb.org/prayer -and-worship/prayers-and-devotions/saints/the-saintly-life-of -edith-stein-st-teresa-benedicta-of-the-cross-and-solidarity.

5. John A. Coleman, "Edith Stein," America: The Jesuit Review, August 8, 2012, https://www.americamagazine.org/content/all -things-edith-stein?gclid=EAIaIQobChMInvn6yIXj8QIVw52GC h3X1QSfEAMYAyAAEgKVwvD_BwE.

CLARA SWAIN

1. Maina Chawla Singh, "Women, Mission, and Medicine: Clara Swain, Anna Kugler, and Early Medical Endeavors in Colonial India," International Bulletin of Missionary Research 29, no. 3 (July 2005): 128–33, http://www.internationalbulletin.org /issues/2005-03/2005-03-128-singh.pdf.

2. Dorothy Clarke Wilson, *Palace of Healing* (Copyright 1968 by Dorothy Clarke Wilson, Kindle version).

3. "History," Clara Swain Hospital, http://www.cshbareilly.com /pages/about-us/history.html.

4. Wilson, *Palace of Healing*, 19.

JONI EARECKSON TADA

1. "Our History," Joni & Friends, https://www.joniandfriends.org /about/our-history/.

2. "Our History."

3. Joni Eareckson Tada, Place of Healing: Wrestling with the Mysteries of Suffering, Pain, and God's Sovereignty (Colorado Springs: David C. Cook, 2010), 20.

4. Tada, Place of Healing.

5. Joni Eareckson Tada, *Joni: An Unforgettable Story* (Nashville: Zondervan, 2001), Kindle edition.

JAMES HUDSON TAYLOR

1. "Hudson Taylor," Christianity Today, https://www. christianitytoday.com/history/people/missionaries/hudson -taylor.html.

2. "Hudson Taylor."

3. "Hudson Taylor."
4. "First China Inland Mission, Now OMF International," OMF International, https://omf.org/us/about/our-story/china-inland-mission/.
5. Warren W. Wiersbe, *50 People Every Christian Should Know* (Grand Rapids: Baker Books, 2009), 133.

ALEXANDER WALTERS

1. Devin Engledew, "Bishop Alexander Walters (1858–1917)," Black Past, March 12, 2007, https://www.blackpast.org/african-american-history/walters-bishop-alexander-1858-1917/.
2. Femi Lewis, "Bishop Alexander Walters: Religious Leader and Civil Rights Activist," ThoughtCo., July 3, 2019, https://www.thoughtco.com/bishop-alexander-walters-biography-3961111.
3. Alexander Walters, *My Life and Work* (New York: Fleming H. Revell, 1917).

ISAAC WATTS

1. "Isaac Watts," Christianity Today, https://www.christianitytoday.com/history/people/poets/isaac-watts.html.
2. "Isaac Watts."
3. "Isaac Watts."

SUSANNA WESLEY

1. DeRusha, *50 Women*, 94.
2. "Susanna Wesley: Mother of Methodism," United Methodist Church, November 22, 2018, https://www.umc.org/en/content/susanna-wesley-mother-of-methodism.
3. DeRusha, *50 Women*, 95.
4. "Susanna Wesley: Mother of Methodism."
5. DeRusha, *50 Women*, 96.

PHILLIS WHEATLEY

1. DeRusha, *50 Women*, 106–7.
2. DeRusha, *50 Women*, 110.
3. "17 Phillis Wheatley Quotes from the First African-American to Publish Poems," Kidadl, https://kidadl.com/articles/phillis-wheatley-quotes-from-the-first-african-american-to-publish-poems.

JOHN WYCLIFFE

1. "John Wycliff," *Christianity Today*, https://www.christianitytoday.com/history/people/moversandshakers/john-wycliffe.html.
2. "John Wycliff," *Christianity Today*.
3. Richard Cavendish, "John Wycliffe Condemned as a Heretic," History Today, May 2015, https://www.historytoday.com/archive/john-wycliffe-condemned-heretic.
4. Galli and Olsen, *131 Christians Everyone Should Know*, 213.
5. Cavendish, "John Wycliffe Condemned as a Heretic."
6. Galli and Olsen, *131 Christians Everyone Should Know*, 211.

LOUIS ZAMPERINI

1. Laura Hillenbrand, Unbroken: A World War II Story of Survival, Resilience, and Redemption (New York: Random House, 2010), 5.
2. John Meroney, "'World War II Isn't Over': Talking to Unbroken Veteran Louis Zamperini," The Atlantic, November 11, 2014, https://www.theatlantic.com/politics/archive/2014/11/world-war-ii-isnt-over-talking-to-unbroken-veteran-louis-zamperini/382616/.
3. Meroney, "'World War II Isn't Over.'"
4. Louis Zamperini, Devil at My Heels: A Heroic Olympian's Astonishing Story of Survival as a Japanese POW in World War II (New York: HarperCollins, 2011), 288–289.